STUDIO & STATE

The Laverys and the Anglo-Irish Treaty

A National Museum of Ireland
and Hugh Lane Gallery exhibition

First published in 2021 by the National Museum of Ireland
In association with the Wordwell Group and Hugh Lane Gallery

First Edition

National Museum of Ireland
Ard-Mhúsaem na hÉireann
Collins Barracks
Benburb Street
Dublin 7
Ireland
www.museum.ie

Wordwell Group
Unit 9, 78 Furze Road
Sandyford
Dublin 18
www.wordwellbooks.com

ISBN: 978-1-914470-01-1

A CIP catalogue record of this book is available from the National Library of Ireland, the British Library and the Library of Congress.

Designed by Yvonne Doherty
Copyedited by Emer Condit
Printed by Gráficas Castuera, Spain

Image page iii:
Fig. 1: E.O. Hoppé: *Hazel, Lady Lavery, and Sir John Lavery*, 1922, reproduced in *Camera*, January 1924. Hugh Lane Gallery Archive

Image page iv:
Fig. 2: Sir John Lavery in his Studio (1919) by Bassano Ltd. National Portrait Gallery, London

Sir John Lavery R.A.
Lady Lavery
"Cunera"
Jan 1924
Photo. E.O. Hoppé

Contents

Fig. 3: Hugh Lane Gallery

Fig. 4: National Museum of Ireland — Decorative Arts & History, Location of the exhibition *Studio & State: The Laverys and the Anglo-Irish Treaty*

Studio & State: The Laverys and the Anglo-Irish Treaty is the culmination of a unique collaboration between Hugh Lane Gallery and the National Museum of Ireland. It commemorates and explores a momentous historic event, the signing of the Anglo-Irish Treaty in 1921, from political, social and cultural perspectives. Our Decade of Centenaries has presented exciting opportunities to revisit the history of this period through multiple disciplines. The collections of the National Museum of Ireland and Hugh Lane Gallery, objects and paintings, provide one such focal point for this exploration. Supported by new research, this exhibition provides in-depth insights into the events which led to the signing of the Treaty and the subsequent interpretations and impacts. *Studio & State* explores a space where the craft of the early twentieth-century artist and statesman merge. It offers us new understandings of the thinking of the key individuals involved and their expectations of how history would view their actions.

In 1921, John Lavery's studio at 5 Cromwell Place, London, his place of process and production, was a centre of Anglo-Irish diplomacy. In an enlightened decision, encouraged by his wife Hazel to 'do something for your country', he set out to paint the portraits of the Irish and British delegates. These portraits, donated by the artist to Hugh Lane Gallery, are a unique and invaluable part of the visual history of the birth of Modern Ireland. For the first time they come together with the illuminating contemporary artefacts from the collections of the National Museum of Ireland.

We would like to thank especially all of the contributors to this publication, whose essays give a further depth of insight into the key themes and works within the exhibition. We are also grateful to the lenders to the exhibition—the National Gallery of Ireland, National Museums Northern Ireland and the Military Archives, Defence Forces Ireland—whose loans enrich the selection of works from Hugh Lane Gallery and the National Museum of Ireland. A special note of thanks to Dr Edith Andrees and Logan Sisley for their expert curation and collaboration on both the exhibition and this accompanying publication. This interdisciplinary approach brings insights and interplays that may otherwise be overlooked and offers opportunity for new avenues of research and understanding of this important historical event 100 years on.

Barbara Dawson, Director, Hugh Lane Gallery &
Lynn Scarff, Director, National Museum of Ireland

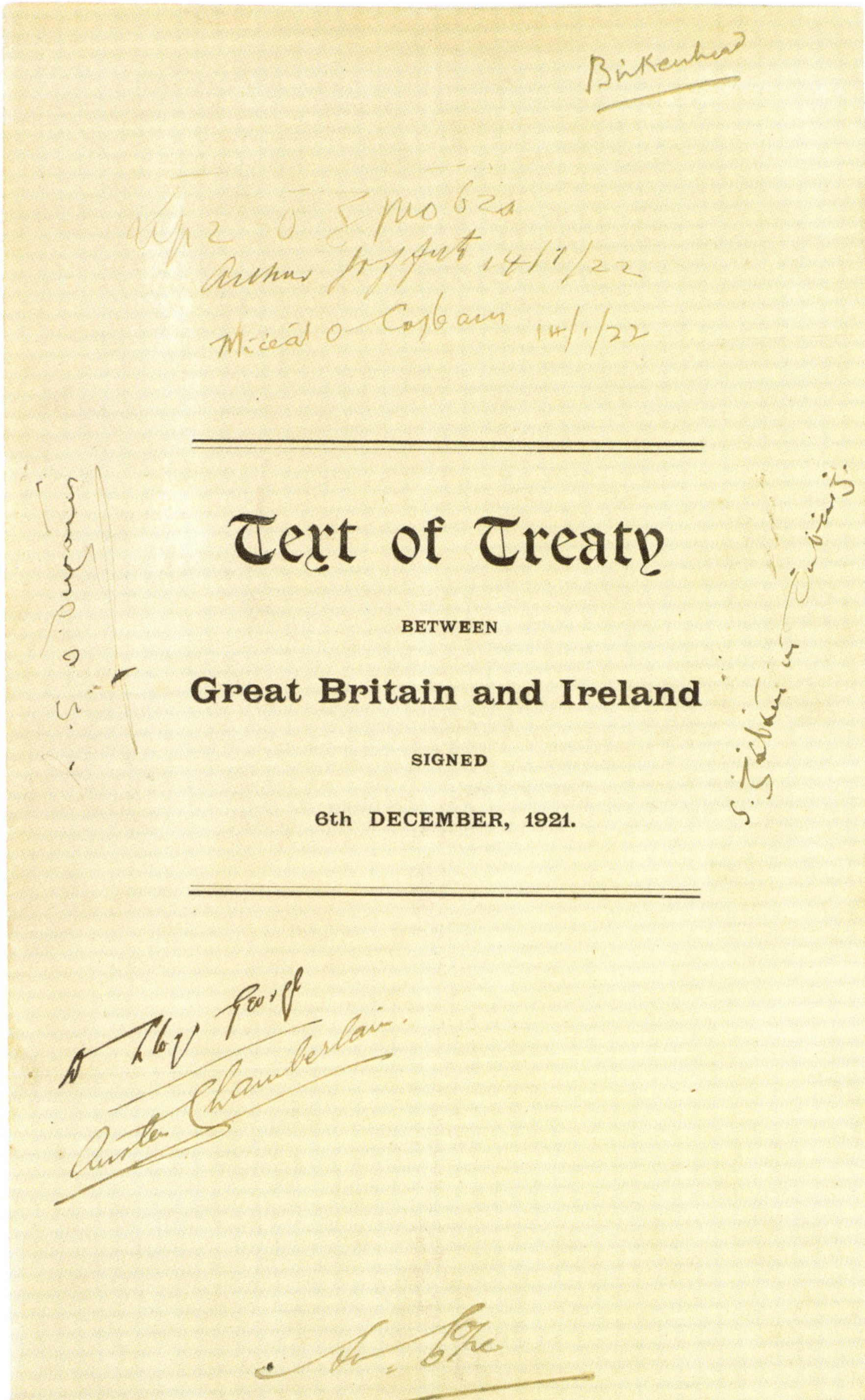

Text of Treaty

BETWEEN

Great Britain and Ireland

SIGNED

6th DECEMBER, 1921.

Fig. 5: Autographed copy of the 1921 Anglo-Irish Treaty

Introducing *Studio & State: The Laverys and the Anglo-Irish Treaty* at the National Museum of Ireland

Edith Andrees

One hundred years ago, in December 1921, a group of twelve men signed the *Articles of Agreement for a Treaty Between Great Britain and Ireland* in London, a bilateral political agreement that had a huge impact on Irish society and has influenced Irish politics and Anglo-Irish relations ever since. The exhibition *Studio & State: The Laverys and the Anglo-Irish Treaty* marks the centenary of this historic event. It combines, for the first time, John Lavery's paintings of the Treaty signatories from the collections of the Hugh Lane Gallery with contemporaneous documents and objects held in the historical collections of the National Museum of Ireland (NMI).

Studio & State is part of the National Museum of Ireland's programme for the Decade of Centenaries 2012–2023. The exhibition follows a long tradition at the NMI of addressing key events in Ireland's political history. Recent examples include a display in 2019 about the 'First Dáil' entitled *Marching on the Road to Freedom: Dáil Éireann 1919*, *Proclaiming a Republic: The 1916 Easter Rising* (2016–20) and new displays in the *Irish Wars 1919–1923* gallery, which opened in 2020 in the permanent exhibition *Soldiers & Chiefs*. With these exhibitions, the National Museum's aim is to re-interrogate historical events from fresh perspectives, using its historical collections as well as loaned material.

This exhibition also continues an ongoing exploration by the Hugh Lane Gallery of the role that art plays in the construction and reimagining of historical narratives. This has been realised in part through re-presentations of the gallery's historic collections, such as *Sir John Lavery: Passion and Politics* (2010), *Revolutionary States: Home Rule and Modern Ireland* (2012), *Dublin Divided: September 1913* (2013) and *High Treason: Roger Casement* (2016). Contemporary artists have also been invited to respond to themes arising from the Decade of Centenaries. These include *Jesse Jones: NO MORE FUN AND GAMES* (2016), which addressed the question of gender equality in the construction and commemoration of history, *Alan Phelan: Our Kind* (2016), which imagined an alternative future for Roger Casement, and *Amanda Dunsmore: Keeper* (2018), which marked the twentieth anniversary of the Good Friday Agreement.

In the case of *Studio & State*, the inclusion of John Lavery's portraits of the Treaty signatories, most of them dating from 1921, allows us to view the Treaty negotiations and related historical documents in the Museum's collection from a different angle—that of the artist's studio, which was not only a place of art production but also one of conversation, entertainment and mediation.

This introduction provides an overview of the exhibition, its aims and intentions, and the Museum objects displayed in it. It will highlight cornerstones of historical narration at work in museums and how this may help us to understand the Anglo-Irish Treaty and what happened at the time of its negotiation and ratification in 1921/1922.

At its core, *Studio & State* highlights John and Hazel Lavery's involvement in Anglo-Irish politics, art and history-making. What was the extent of their influence in the context of the Anglo-Irish Treaty negotiations? What rendered their home a 'neutral ground'[1] as they proposed? In devising *Studio & State*, the exhibition team was working on the understanding that negotiations for and the signing of the Anglo-Irish Treaty were crystallising moments for Ireland in the twentieth century, continuing their influence on Irish politics and society to this day. The Treaty can be viewed as one of the many symbolic places in which collective Irish memories crystallise, a central 'place of memory' or *lieu de mémoire,* as defined by French historian Pierre Nora in the 1980s.[2] The Treaty was both a vehicle of peace, concluding the Irish War of Independence (1919–21), and, as it turned out, a catalyst for civil war.

The exhibition explores events between July 1921, when the Truce was agreed in Dublin, and January 1922, when the Anglo-Irish Treaty was narrowly ratified in Dáil Éireann. Objects chosen from the National Museum's collections and dating from this time include a copy of the Treaty document autographed by the signatories, the fountain-pen reputedly used by Michael Collins to sign the original Treaty document, and pro- and anti-Treaty propaganda works.

The selected historical documents illustrate two problematic issues during July–December 1921: a near-impasse between the Irish and British on the subject of the status of the new Irish state and divisions within the Irish nationalist movement itself.[3] These divisions become most obvious in the handbills issued by both pro-

Fig. 6: Michael Collins's pen, reputedly used to sign the Anglo-Irish Treaty, December 1921

Treaty and anti-Treaty sides in 1922. Used as information, election and propaganda material, they outline respective goals and—in often sharp and damning language—describe the motives of the opposing political side. They also point—at least from our present perspective—to the ensuing Civil War (June 1922–May 1923).

In combining the Museum's historical documents and photographs with John Lavery's portraits of Treaty signatories on both the Irish and British sides, we hope to highlight the particular complexities of this time and the diversity of the personalities involved in the negotiations. At first glance, the portraits display a relative uniformity and belie the intense difference in convictions held by the portrayed, including the disagreements among the Irish delegation. The selected historical documents illustrate how Irish people involved in politics in 1921–2 strove together to achieve political independence, but also where they differed and eventually split.

Fig. 7: Arthur Griffith arriving at the Mansion House for the Anglo-Irish Truce negotiations, 8 July 1921

Fig. 8: Éamon de Valera (centre) arriving at the Mansion House, Dublin, July 1921

The long shadows cast in Ireland by the political split after the ratification of the Treaty have begun to blur and be transformed. As our temporal distance from the historical events of 1921–2 increases, it arguably gets easier to discuss them and embed them in a historical narrative. This is partly because the events leading to the ratification of the Treaty in 1922 are passing from what might be termed collective 'communicative memory' into more formalised 'cultural memory'.[4] According to Jan and Aleida Assmann, communicative memory is 'living memory', as those who personally heard of or experienced the events are still alive to tell the story. It is based on the historical experiences of individuals and is carried on informally through interactions in daily life. Communicative memory reaches back about 80–100 years, as far as the oldest member of a group can reach with their memories or those they heard from older people when growing up. Cultural memory, on the other hand, relates to a more distant past. It refers to events that instil meaning into a group's existence, such as the foundation of a political state. It consists, for example, of texts and images used repeatedly in public spaces and often stored in cultural institutions such as museums and archives.[5] In the museum setting, both communicative and cultural memory inform one another. Historical narratives in exhibitions support orally transmitted accounts, which are often connected to the objects we collect and display.

Nevertheless, a gap between experienced and narrated time remains. The original life context of the Treaty negotiations is now lost and we examine and tell its stories retrospectively, from the end-point, not through immediate experience. How fortunate, then, that there are fascinating objects in the collections of the National Museum of Ireland, the Hugh Lane Gallery and other cultural institutions which can serve as 'triggers' of memory and help us rebuild some of this original life context.[6] In the case of the *Studio & State* exhibition these include paintings, handbills, Treaty documents, photographs and historical film footage. Encountering these objects may simultaneously be an 'experience of strangeness and an act of familiarisation'.[7] Every generation adjusts existing historical narratives that are deemed relevant until they seem to represent—from the present perspective of the narrators—'lived-through experience'.[8]

Incompleteness is, of course, an inherent characteristic of historical narration. The development of any story is accompanied by a selection process. It is impossible to exhibit a definitive account of the Treaty and its background, its consequences and its legacy in a single gallery space. Even with our focus on John and Hazel Lavery, the artist's studio and portraits of the signatories, we had to further narrow down what would go on display on this occasion. This selection was based not only on resource considerations such as space but also on the objects that survive

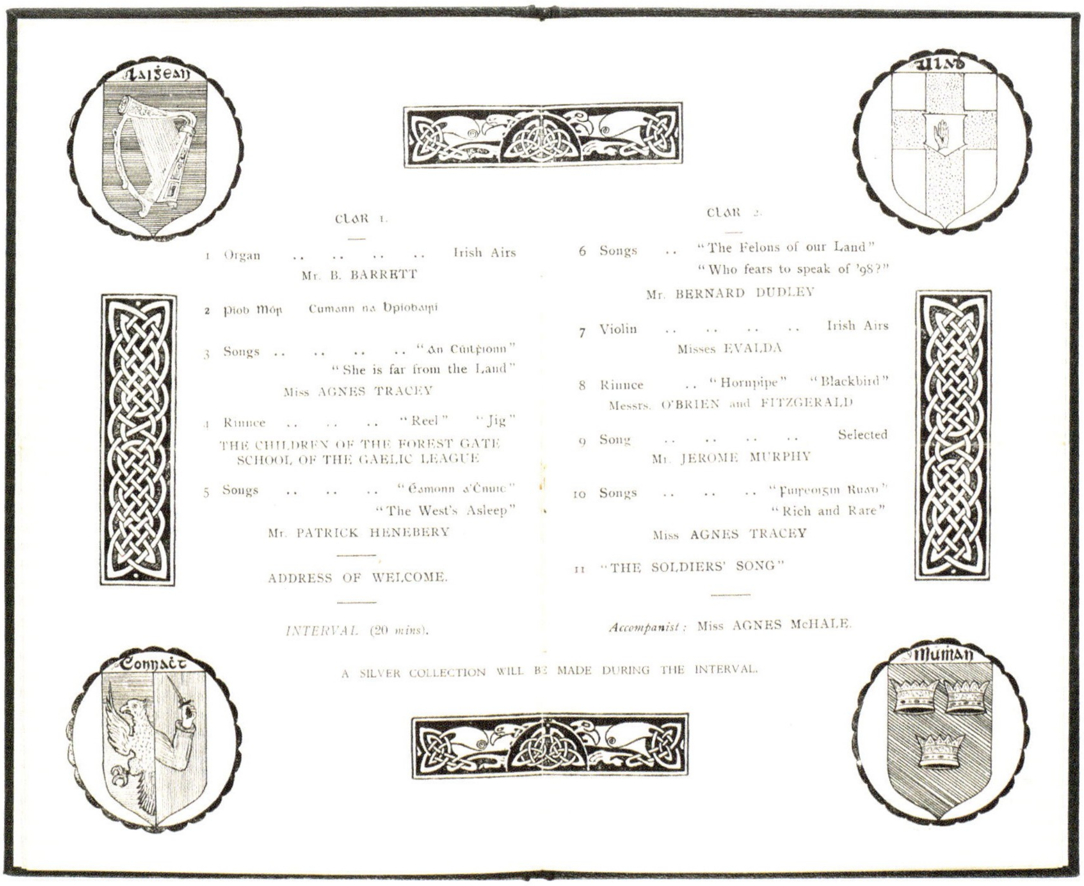

Laiġean

Ulaḋ

CLÁR 1.

1 Organ .. .. Irish Airs
Mr. B. BARRETT

2 Píob Mór Cumann na bPíobairí

3 Songs .. .. "An Cúilḟionn"
"She is far from the Land"
Miss AGNES TRACEY

4 Rinnce .. .. .. "Reel" "Jig"
THE CHILDREN OF THE FOREST GATE SCHOOL OF THE GAELIC LEAGUE

5 Songs .. .. .. "Éamonn a'Ċnuic"
"The West's Asleep"
Mr. PATRICK HENEBERY

ADDRESS OF WELCOME.

INTERVAL (20 mins).

CLÁR 2.

6 Songs .. "The Felons of our Land"
"Who fears to speak of '98?"
Mr. BERNARD DUDLEY

7 Violin .. .. Irish Airs
Misses EVALDA

8 Rinnce .. "Hornpipe" "Blackbird"
Messrs. O'BRIEN and FITZGERALD

9 Song .. .. Selected
Mr. JEROME MURPHY

10 Songs .. .. .. "Fuireoigín Ruaḋ"
"Rich and Rare"
Miss AGNES TRACEY

11 "THE SOLDIERS' SONG"

Accompanist: Miss AGNES McHALE.

A SILVER COLLECTION WILL BE MADE DURING THE INTERVAL.

Connaċt

Muṁan

Fig. 9: Programme performed at the Royal Albert Hall for the Irish Treaty delegation, October 1921

in museum collections. Documents and paper-based material dominate the NMI collections relating to the Treaty. We have attempted to place the more formal documents alongside objects that bear witness to activities that took place outside the negotiation rooms. A lunch menu, a souvenir programme of a concert at the Royal Albert Hall put on for the Irish delegates, and a roulette wheel and gaming sheet used during breaks from the arduous task of negotiating such a monumental treaty give further glimpses into the delegates' time in London in the summer and autumn of 1921. We will never fully know what it was like to live then, 100 years ago, with the ideals and hopes that the Treaty delegates held.

The limits of historical narration notwithstanding, the exhibition offers a new angle to that past and opens up fascinating connections between art and historical interpretations of that time. In terms of historical evidence, it does so from a predominantly Irish perspective. This is due to our starting-point: the historical collection of the National Museum of Ireland largely reflects what happened in *Ireland* prior to the signing of the Treaty and in its aftermath. The objects either are directly related to the Irish delegations or show what was decided and voted on by people living in Ireland and identifying as belonging (in their many different ways) to this place. Most of the exhibited documents—and even Lavery's portraits—were produced for public display in Ireland.

The objects are displayed in loose chronological order to shed some light on specific events between July 1921 and January 1922. The truce of July 1921, the Treaty negotiations in London and the debates in Ireland after it was signed are the three key areas highlighted using museum objects. John Lavery's portraits of the signatories take centre stage in the gallery space and 'interact' with written notes, documents and historical photographs depicting their contemporaries. Thus, by extension, *Studio & State* is about the people who negotiated and proposed the Treaty, who argued for and against it. It is about their encounters, their exchanges and their aspirations, as expressed in imagery and written documents. It sheds light on the wrangling and assuredness of the time, coupled with a sense of enormous uncertainty and risk.

Examination of the autograph books, letters and personal notes in the National Museum's collection from that time makes it quite clear that the plenipotentiaries were aware of the long-lasting impact of this Anglo-Irish Treaty. There was an acute sense that they were bearing witness to what would become a historically monumental event. John Lavery's role as an artist chronicling and interpreting historical events and personalities did not begin with the Treaty negotiations; neither did Hazel's involvement and support in this endeavour, as Sinéad McCoole outlines in this publication.[9] Both John and Hazel were witnesses of the historical events in 1921 and residues of their 'lived-through experience' linger in the portraits, which John Lavery donated to the Municipal Gallery of Modern Art Dublin (now Hugh Lane Gallery) in 1935.

Most of the NMI material on display was collected from the 1930s onwards, reflecting the Museum's institutional and collecting history. The National Museum originated from a number of different collections, which were merged when it was founded as the Dublin Museum of Science and Art in 1877. The Department of Science and Art in London ran the Museum with the aim of furthering science and art education within the British Empire.[10] Count George N. Plunkett (who was later a member of the first Irish Treaty delegation, which headed to London in July 1921) became the Museum's Director in 1907. He stated that the Museum should have a 'collection of things distinctively Irish, both ancient and modern'.[11] Thus, although the reshaping of the Dublin Museum of Science and Art into a national Irish institution took place well before political independence was won, it did not start out as a national history museum as we may understand such a thing in the 21st century.[12] After the foundation of the Irish Free State in 1922, a renewed focus on the Irish antiquities collection and the collecting of Irish ethnological objects became more pronounced.

Some items on display in the *Studio & State* exhibition were purchased, but much of the material has been donated to the NMI by friends, acquaintances or relatives (often surviving wives or sisters) of those who took part in the struggle for independence. It is not surprising, then, that much of the surviving material was donated in the 1940s and later, when living memory of the event began to wane. Through objects we create legacy and meaning. The many objects gifted to the Museum emphasise the wish that something may endure, that they may help us to remember events and, most of all, those who came before. They are also a powerful reminder that we should not take the *status quo* for granted. For us today, museum objects offer a chance to catch a glimpse of a tumultuous past in which we have not participated ourselves at first hand. They remind us of the goals of people living in Ireland 100 years ago. While we are always physically situated in the present when examining objects and assembling historical narratives, we can also imagine a collective future from this perspective. How do we want Ireland to be remembered in 100 years' time? What should have changed, and what should be protected?

The essays in this publication can be read alongside the exhibition or independently of it. They offer a more detailed exploration of the historical events of 100 years ago, as well as responses to John Lavery's portraits from contemporary artists. Fearghal McGarry takes us back to the Treaty negotiations and gives detailed historical context to the portraits. Logan Sisley examines Lavery's Treaty portraits, their reception and journey into the Hugh Lane Gallery collection. His and Sinéad McCoole's essays interrogate, with different emphasis, the studio space in addition to Hazel and John Lavery's intentions and connections with the British and Irish political élites and delegates at the time of the Treaty negotiations. Fintan Cullen's essay invites us to take a closer look at Lavery's portraits and their place in Irish cultural history. Mick O'Dea, David Godbold and Niamh McCann explore the portraits and the Anglo-

Irish Treaty from their personal perspectives as contemporary practising artists 100 years on. Finally, we have included a fully annotated listing of all paintings and objects on display in the exhibition, including images and generous loans from the National Gallery of Ireland, National Museums Northern Ireland and the Irish Military Archives.

Fig. 10: Typewriter with Irish lettering used to type letters to the British government in 1921

Endnotes

1 John Lavery, *The life of a painter* (Boston, 1940), p. 208.

2 Pierre Nora and Lawrence D. Kritzman (eds), *Realms of memory* (Columbia University Press, 1996). English translation of part of Nora's original French publication *Les lieux de mémoire*.

3 Michael Laffan, *The resurrection of Ireland: the Sinn Féin Party 1916–1923* (Cambridge, 1999), p. 353. Liam Weeks, Mícheál Ó Fathartaigh, *The Treaty. Debating and establishing the Irish state* (Newbridge, 2018).

4 Jan Assmann, *Das kulturelle Gedächtnis. Schrift, Erinnerung und politische Identität in frühen Hochkulturen* (München, 1992). Jan and Aleida Assmann are leading German theorists in the field of memory studies and have examined how collectives remember the past. For essays on collective memory and 'places of memory' in the Irish context, see Ian McBride (ed.), *History and memory in modern Ireland* (Cambridge, 2001).

5 An excellent summary of Jan and Aleida Assmann's concept is given in Astrid Erll, *Kollektives Gedächtnis und Erinnerungskulturen* (Stuttgart, 2005), pp 27–33. See also Jan Assmann, 'Kollektives Gedächtnis und kulturelle Identität', in Jan Assmann and Tonio Hölscher (eds), *Kultur und Gedächtnis* (Frankfurt am Main, 1988), pp 9–19.

6 Aleida Assmann, *Erinnerungsräume. Formen und Wandlungen des kulturellen Gedächtnisses* (München, 1999).

7 Alon Confino, *Germany as a culture of remembrance. Promises and limits of writing history* (Chapel Hill, 2006), p. 6.

8 See Polkinhorne's essay on narrative psychology and historical awareness: Donald E. Polkinhorne, 'Narrative Psychologie und Geschichtsbewuβtsein. Beziehungen und Perspektiven', in Jürgen Straub (ed.), *Erzählung, Identität und Historisches Bewuβtsein* (Frankfurt am Main, 1998), p. 23.

9 See also Sinéad McCoole, *Hazel. A life of Lady Lavery, 1880–1935* (Dublin, 2016).

10 Elizabeth Crooke, *Politics, archaeology and the creation of a National Museum of Ireland* (Dublin, 2000).

11 *Ibid.*, p. 138.

12 Simon Knell, Peter Aronsson and Aron Bugge Amundsen (eds), *National Museums: new studies from around the world* (London, 2011).

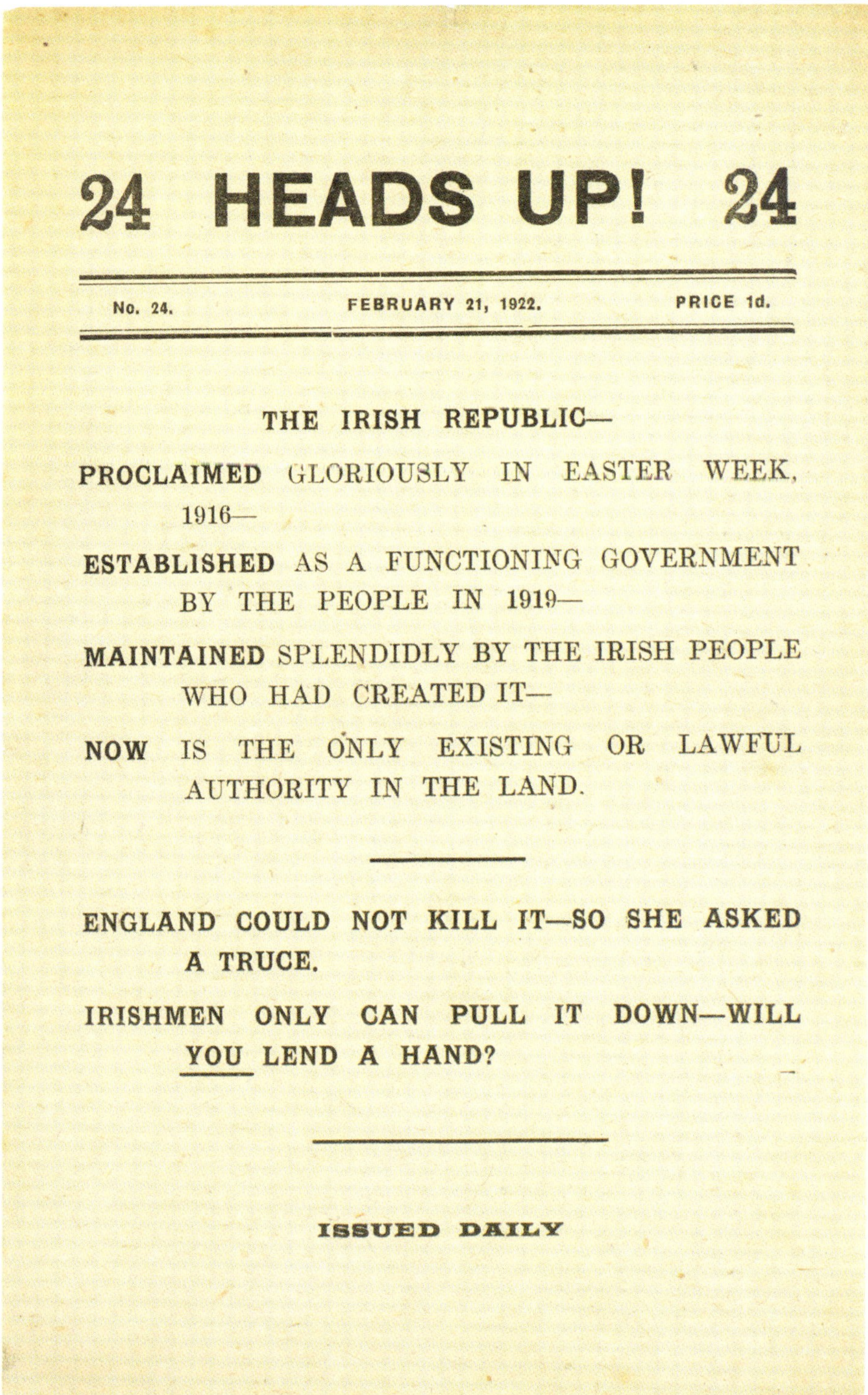

24 HEADS UP! 24

No. 24. FEBRUARY 21, 1922. PRICE 1d.

THE IRISH REPUBLIC—

PROCLAIMED GLORIOUSLY IN EASTER WEEK, 1916—

ESTABLISHED AS A FUNCTIONING GOVERNMENT BY THE PEOPLE IN 1919—

MAINTAINED SPLENDIDLY BY THE IRISH PEOPLE WHO HAD CREATED IT—

NOW IS THE ONLY EXISTING OR LAWFUL AUTHORITY IN THE LAND.

ENGLAND COULD NOT KILL IT—SO SHE ASKED A TRUCE.

IRISHMEN ONLY CAN PULL IT DOWN—WILL YOU LEND A HAND?

ISSUED DAILY

Fig. 11: Anti-Treaty handbill, 1922

Uimh. 19

DHÁ BHLIAIN Ó SHIN DOB IONANN

Saorstát na hEireann

agus

Saoirse na hEireann

Anois, dar le Childers agus le "Gaedhil" eile dá shórt is ionann é agus

DAOIRSE na hEIREANN

an rud díreach a theastuigheann ó Shasana.

Cé thógfaidh focal an tSasanaigh thar focal an Eireannaigh ar cad is

SAOIRSE

ann

BHÓTÁIL LEIS AN

SAORSTÁT.

Páipeur Gaedhlach, Dubhach Gaedhlach, Saothar Ceárd-Chumainn Ghaedhlaigh.

Fig. 12: Pro-Treaty handbill, 1922

‘The Ideal of Freedom’: the Anglo-Irish Treaty

Fearghal McGarry

Whether Irish revolutionaries viewed the Anglo-Irish Treaty signed on 6 December 1921 as enabling national self-government or as a betrayal of the Irish Republic, they were agreed on its disastrous consequences. The divisive settlement destroyed the unity of the republican movement, portending a traumatic descent into fraternal violence. The Sinn Féin propagandist Frank Gallagher spoke for many when he described the Treaty as marking the end of the ‘Four Glorious Years’.[1] The Cork writer Seán Ó Faoláin recalled how its subtle abstractions were interpreted by his comrades who had courageously dedicated themselves to a hitherto undefined ideal of national freedom:

> we began to wonder, to discuss, to argue crossly, and finally to quarrel bitterly over what each of us might mean, and all must agree to mean, by such unfamiliar terms as association, external association, oath of recognition … or even of allegiance to a head or to the headship of an association, and so on, blinded and dazzled as we were by our ikons, caught in the labyrinth of our dearest symbols—our Ancient Past, our Broken Chains, our Seven

> Centuries of Slavery, the Silenced Harp, the Glorious Dead, the tears of Dark Rosaleen, the miseries of the Poor Old Woman, the Sunburst of Freedom that we had always believed would end our Long Night and solve all our problems with the descent of a heavenly-human order which we would immediately recognise as the reality of our never-articulated dreams.[2]

The perspective provided by the centenary of the Treaty and the more recent fading of the Civil War political alignments that resulted from it offer an opportunity for a more detached understanding of why arcane differences over rival formulations of sovereignty produced such a devastating outcome. This essay assesses the circumstances leading to the truce of July 1921 and the course of the negotiations that followed. It evaluates the Treaty and the parliamentary debates that saw its ratification. The conclusion briefly considers the contested memory and legacy of a settlement that, for all its importance, generated little enthusiasm on either side of the Irish Sea.

I

By the early summer of 1921 neither the republican leadership nor the British government had much appetite for further conflict. Although Volunteers in the strongest fighting areas in south-west Ireland were confident in their ability to extend their guerrilla campaign, their Dublin-based leadership was more aware of the IRA's vulnerabilities. For the more politically attuned within Sinn Féin, it was unclear what gains might result from further violence. Meanwhile, important organs of nationalist opinion such as the Catholic Church, press and business interests clamoured for peace.

In Britain public and political opinion had shifted since late 1920, when Prime Minister David Lloyd George claimed 'to have murder by the throat'. Despite an increasingly effective counter-insurrectionary campaign that saw the capture of over 5,000 republicans, press reports of 'Black and Tan' and Auxiliary brutality tarnished Britain's reputation, particularly in the United States and the Dominions. Global coverage of the death of hunger striker Terence MacSwiney, the killing of civilians on Bloody Sunday and the burning of Cork city undermined Britain's moral authority abroad and led to disquiet on the home front. General Sir Nevil Macready, who commanded British troops in Ireland, impressed on the Cabinet the necessity for even greater ruthlessness to subdue the IRA.

Critically, the creation of a unionist-controlled jurisdiction in Ulster from the autumn of 1920 as a result of the Government of Ireland Act altered the political calculus at Westminster. The partition of Ireland enabled Lloyd George, a Liberal whose position rested on the support of his majority coalition partners in the staunchly unionist Conservative Party, to hold out the prospect of a more generous settlement for Southern Ireland. As Tory hard-liner Andrew Bonar Law observed: 'I would give the South anything or almost anything, but I would not attempt to force anything on Ulster'.[3] Against this background, King George V's conciliatory speech at the opening of the Northern Irish parliament in Belfast in June 1921 proved sufficient to end the stalemate in Ireland.

The sudden announcement of the truce disoriented combatants on all sides. Ernie O'Malley, commander of the IRA's 2nd Southern Division in Munster, described his surprise when a boy up from Dublin delivered a terse order announcing the suspension of active operations from 11 July:

> We sat down to talk about the news in wonder. What did it mean? And why had senior officers no other information than a bald message? Would the Truce last a week, or perhaps two weeks? We were willing to keep up the pressure which had been increasing steadily ... And so ended for us what we called the scrap; the people later on, the trouble; and others, fond of labels, the Revolution.[4]

The truce provoked jubilation, consternation and suspicion. Although popular, not least with the public, the ceasefire's implications were resented by the hawkish and zealous: any future settlement would inevitably fall short of passionately advocated objectives. Sinn Féin leaders, such as Michael Collins, who had publicly advanced an unyielding republican line—'Compromises are difficult and settle nothing'—began to disclose their more flexible private positions: 'No one has ever defined a republic'.[5] It was only after the truce that Éamon de Valera told the Dáil, 'We are not doctrinaire republicans'.[6] This came as unwelcome news to some of his own followers. Returning from the United States, Mary MacSwiney was alarmed by the 'atmosphere of what I can only call compromise. I was told to the right and left of me that we could not possibly get a Republic.'[7]

Within the British establishment, many were equally dismayed by the truce's humiliating implication of equality between a great world power and a movement previously denounced as a 'murder gang'. The terms of the truce were particularly resented in Northern Ireland, where the Ulster Special Constabulary was temporarily demobilised but the IRA was recognised through the institution of military liaison arrangements. Unionist anxiety about betrayal from London fuelled renewed sectarian violence in Ulster. The truce held in the South but drinking, lax discipline and an influx of 'trucileers' eroded IRA morale.[8]

Both sides' reluctance to concede political ground resulted in three months of sparring until de Valera accepted Lloyd George's invitation that an Irish delegation travel to London to determine 'how the association of Ireland with the community of nations known as the British Empire may best be reconciled with Irish national aspirations'.[9] It was the first of many elegant formulations aimed at surmounting the seemingly irreconcilable demands of republicans and imperialists.

Fig. 13: Members of the Irish Treaty delegation and staff on their way to London, October 1921

II

The make-up of the Irish delegation reflected the divergent factions and political perspectives within the republican movement. Arthur Griffith, minister for foreign affairs and deputy leader of Sinn Féin, chaired the delegation. The other key negotiator was Michael Collins, who—as minister for finance, IRB president and IRA director of intelligence—commanded broad support across the republican movement. The staunchly republican Robert Barton and Erskine Childers (a secretary rather than a delegate) were chosen by de Valera to counterbalance the more flexible Griffith and Collins. Lawyers Éamonn Duggan and George Gavan Duffy were dismissed by de Valera as 'legal padding'.[10] Revealingly, no women were appointed as delegates.

The glaring omission was de Valera himself. At the time, and over the course of his long career, de Valera provided various explanations for his decision to remain in Dublin. These ranged from the symbolic (as the embodiment of the Republic, he, like King George V, should remain above political entanglements) to the tactical (his presence in Dublin would keep in check Cabinet hard-liners such as Cathal Brugha, and provide the basis for a last-ditch initiative should the talks collapse). Although still close to de Valera, Collins feared that he and Griffith were being 'set up' to take the blame for the unpalatable compromises that would accompany any settlement.[11] Ominously, the negotiations coincided with a broader series of disputes, including a poisonous row triggered by the Cabinet's efforts to assert its authority over the IRA, 'which gradually fractured the solidarity of the republican leadership'.[12] Such tensions reflected personal and factional rivalries that would influence the subsequent Treaty split.

These unpropitious circumstances help to explain the inconsistent guidance given to the delegation. Although appointed as plenipotentiaries, thereby enjoying the right to 'negotiate and conclude' a treaty, they were instructed to seek Cabinet approval before reaching any final agreement. The question of whether they had the authority to sign an agreement would become one of the most contested issues in the Treaty debates. The negotiators were poorly supported from home, and there remained considerable confusion over what the Cabinet considered an acceptable bottom line. While de Valera insisted to the plenipotentiaries that external association—an ambiguous concept based on voluntary association with the British Empire—was achievable, there was little support for this subtle proposal from either doctrinaire republicans or, more pertinently, the British negotiators. De Valera's efforts to steer the negotiations from Dublin deepened divisions both within the delegation and between the delegation and the Cabinet. Indicative of the atmosphere of suspicion enveloping the talks, Childers was soon reporting back to de Valera on the negotiations, while Griffith and Collins were meeting with British negotiators without the knowledge of the other plenipotentiaries.[13]

The Irish envoys faced experienced and talented negotiators such as Winston Churchill, Austen Chamberlain and Lord Birkenhead, who skilfully exploited these divisions. Lloyd George assessed the Irish delegates as having 'none of the skill of the old nationalists; these men are not accustomed to finessing'.[14] Although divisions existed among the British delegation, which included Liberals and Tories who had clashed intensely over Ireland before the First World War, they had a clearer sense of their objectives and how to achieve them. Revealingly, the Irish delegates failed to present an alternative position paper at the outset of the talks, ensuring that the course of the negotiations was shaped by the British agenda.

The negotiations focused on territorial unity, the role of the Crown and Ireland's relationship with the Empire. Both sides prioritised sovereignty. For many republicans, full membership of the Empire and the swearing of an oath to the monarch were incompatible with independence. For the British negotiators, anything short of this was politically unacceptable, not least because of its implications for the unity of the wider Empire. The British delegation sought to avoid a breakdown of the talks on Ulster, where, Lloyd George conceded, they had 'a very weak case'. As the influential civil servant Tom Jones observed: 'Men will die for throne and Empire. I do not know who will die for Tyrone and Fermanagh.'[15]

The Irish delegates, for their part, understood the need to attribute any failure to reach a settlement to irreconcilable differences over Ulster rather than Crown or Empire. Given this symmetry, Ulster emerged as the strategic fulcrum that would shape the outcome of the talks. The Irish delegates signalled their willingness to compromise on sovereignty if Britain gave way on unity. Lloyd George undertook to pressure James Craig, the Northern Irish prime minster, 'to secure essential unity' if the Irish gave way on the vital matters of Crown, Empire and defence.[16] Much would turn over the next months on what constituted essential unity.

The Irish delegates' negotiating missteps have been much analysed. When the talks ground to an impasse, following Lloyd George's realisation that he could not pressure the granite-like Craig to accept Northern Ireland's inclusion in an all-Ireland settlement, the British prime minister—raising the unwelcome spectre of the replacement of his government by a more hard-line Tory administration—proposed an ingenious alternative. If Northern Ireland ultimately refused to 'come under any all-Ireland parliament', Griffith explained to de Valera, Lloyd George would 'set up a Govt. for the 26 Counties with all the promised powers, and appoint a boundary commission to de-limit "Ulster", confining this Ulster to its Partition Act powers. This would give us most of Tyrone, Fermanagh, and part of Armagh, Down, etc.' Griffith's acceptance of this proposal on 9 November allowed 'Lloyd George to wriggle off the horns of his Ulster dilemma'.

The plenipotentiaries' belief, cultivated by Lloyd George, that a boundary commission would render Northern Ireland unviable would prove optimistic, but Griffith's personal undertaking, given privately to Lloyd George, that the Irish delegates would not publicly repudiate the prime minister's proposals on Ulster ensured the British tactical breakthrough. During the fraught denouement of the negotiations in December, Lloyd George's revelation of Griffith's assurance provided the first of two dramatic moments. Frustrated by the Irish delegation's reluctance to close the deal, the frustrated prime minister informed Collins that he would tell his Cabinet that negotiations had broken down over 'the question of "within or without" the Empire'. When Collins instead indicated his dissatisfaction at the proposals on Ulster, Lloyd George produced the memorandum summarising Griffith's acceptance of these provisions. Responding, whether naively or emotionally, to this implication of bad faith, Griffith then announced his willingness to sign the document regardless of whether Craig—or, indeed, his own colleagues—accepted it, a 'monumental mistake that shattered the residual cohesion of the Irish delegation and transformed the chemistry of the negotiations'.

Claiming that he had assumed that Griffith spoke for the delegation as a whole, Lloyd George pressed home his advantage with another theatrical gesture. Insisting that unless all the delegates signed there would be no agreement, he held up two letters that he had drafted to Craig: one stating that the Irish delegates had recommended that the Dáil accept the Treaty, the other reporting the collapse of the negotiations, an outcome that would result in 'war within three days'.[17] After withdrawing to consider their decision, and without consulting Dublin, the delegation returned to 10 Downing Street shortly after 2 a.m. on 6 December to sign the Treaty.

The outcome undoubtedly marked a success for British statecraft. While securing Irish acceptance of Crown and Empire, the settlement permitted Northern Ireland to vote itself out of the Irish Free State, thereby confirming six-county partition (albeit with the position of the final border to be determined by a boundary commission 'in accordance with the wishes of the inhabitants, so far as may be compatible with economic and geographic conditions'). Moreover, Britain's retention of three 'Treaty ports' ruled out the possibility of an independent defence policy in time of war. 'In essentials,' Tom Jones concluded, 'we have given nothing that was not in the July proposals.'[18]

Despite the restrictions on sovereignty, and the failure to reverse (or, more realistically, to modify) the *fait accompli* that was partition, the agreement delivered much for nationalists. 'The story of the negotiations', Charles Townshend has suggested, was the movement of Griffith and Collins 'to a belief that acceptance of symbolic British suzerainty would no longer compromise effective Irish independence'.[19] Providing for 26-county dominion status, it offered far greater powers of self-government than Home Rule, taking the South out of the UK state. The Free State would possess most of the attributes of statehood, including a national army, while a Council of Ireland, in theory at least, allowed for the subsequent reunification of Ireland. Moreover, dominion powers—already substantial—were themselves in transition as the British Empire evolved into the less-hierarchical 'British Commonwealth of Nations', a term whose first legal appearance came in the text of the Treaty. Significant last-minute concessions had been offered by Britain to sweeten the deal, including fiscal and trade autonomy, and the dilution of the oath of allegiance to the Crown to one of fidelity. On both sides of the Irish Sea, however, debate on the Treaty would focus more on its symbolic than its substantial measures.

III

The Treaty divided every republican organisation in Ireland. The rupture began at the top on 8 December when, in a surprising setback for de Valera's authority, the Cabinet voted by four votes to three to recommend the Treaty to the Dáil. The following day, a week before the Dáil was due to debate it, de Valera made public his opposition to the agreement. A statement by the IRA's 1st Southern Division on 10 December, urging the government to reject the Treaty, suggested that many Volunteers would not feel bound by the Dáil's decision. One reason for the extent of the crisis that followed was the weakness of both political and military republican institutions. Comprising 125 Sinn Féin deputies who had been elected unopposed in May 1921, mainly owing to their IRA records, the Second Dáil had no record as a decision-making body. It met infrequently, and excluded non-republican opinion, notably Labour, that would have supported the settlement.

The Treaty was exhaustively debated over thirteen days of public and private sessions between 14 December and 7 January. Much discussion focused on the right of the delegates to sign the Treaty (an arguably moot point) and the Irish Free State's links to the British Crown and Empire. There was little discussion of partition, but this likely reflected the sidelining of the issue by the Boundary Commission, and the lack of any obvious alternative proposal on Ulster, rather than a lack of interest in partition, which had been central to Sinn Féin's repudiation of the Irish Parliamentary Party.

While this preoccupation with symbolic issues (such as the oath and the role of the governor-general as representative of the monarch) has been much criticised, it would have been surprising if the outcome of a conflict centred on sovereignty had not focused on the symbols through which independence was made tangible. Indeed, it could be argued that negotiators on both sides had paid insufficient attention to the importance attached to symbols by their opponents. As Heather Jones has observed, British politicians underestimated the extent to which anti-monarchism had become a defining feature of Irish nationalism after Easter 1916, while republicans did not appreciate the increasingly vital role played by the Crown in binding Britain to its Dominions in its more loosely configured post-war Empire.[20]

Although the Treaty debates indicated a neat cleavage between deputies advocating the settlement as a stepping-stone to independence and those unwilling to disestablish the Republic, the gap between both sides was narrower. Aside from a zealous minority unwilling to contemplate any connection to Britain, the choice was not between the Irish Republic and British Empire—or between 'right and wrong', as the unyielding Mary MacSwiney put it—but between two unsatisfactory compromises. 'Document No. 2', de Valera's proposed alternative, replicated most of the Treaty's provisions, including on Ulster. Despite (or perhaps because of) this, de Valera also framed the clash in misleadingly Manichean terms: 'The people have no right to do wrong'. His awareness that militant republicans did not see much of a distinction between membership of and association with the Empire may explain his insistence that discussion of his document was confined to a private session.

Pro-Treaty arguments were broadly pragmatic: the Treaty was the best deal achievable; it permitted, in Collins's pithy formulation, 'the freedom to achieve freedom'; and there was little alternative other than a return to a conflict that was unlikely to end more favourably. Given the obvious constraints on sovereignty, Treatyite rhetoric was characterised by a defensive tone. Anti-Treaty arguments were more strident, uncompromising and moralistic. Numerous republicans would later concede, as did Ernie O'Malley, 'a certain hardness in our idealism' which 'made us aloof from ordinary living'.[21] The following year W.B. Yeats reflected on the Civil War violence occurring close to his rural Galway tower-house, Thoor Ballylee, in similar terms:

> We had fed the heart on fantasies,
> The heart's grown brutal from the fare,
> More substance in our enmities
> Than in our love ...[22]

Charles Townshend has suggested that those most vehemently opposed to the Treaty 'had mostly been less committed to the task of turning the Republic from an abstract concept into a functioning machine of representative government',[23] but the oft-noted contrast between pragmatism and idealism also reflected how one side was required to defend an actual settlement while the other could hold out the prospect of complete freedom. The frequently asserted claim that the Treaty brought republicans 'into the Empire' reflected the dubious assumption that Ireland had managed to leave it.

Given its momentous consequences, the Treaty split (and the Civil War that followed) has often been characterised as the product of deep ideological divisions or radically contrasting mentalities. Political scientists identified a split between constitutionally minded pragmatists and romantic élitists, 'majority right and divine right', or democrats and 'the cult of the virtuous minority',[24] but the militant, militaristic and authoritarian could also be found among Treaty supporters. Conversely, anti-Treaty leaders such as de Valera would later prove their democratic credentials. The similarities between both sides are more striking than the differences. Remarkably, there is no significant correlation between the Dáil vote on the Treaty and factors such as class, age, occupation, education, economic circumstances, military experience, imprisonment or loss of family members.[25]

With all six female deputies (an admittedly small sample) opposing the Treaty, the most obvious distinction between both sides was that of gender. As four of these women were related to martyred republicans, and because much of their rhetoric was characterised by 'invocations of the dead', it has been argued that they strategically positioned themselves as 'keepers of republican memory' and 'preservers of the revolutionary legacy'.[26] The prominence of women on the anti-Treaty side and as participants in the Civil War gave rise to a misogynistic discourse that not only depicted republican women as embittered and fanatical but also characterised the broader anti-Treaty movement as 'feminine' owing to its emotional and irrational nature. Consequently, the Treaty debates, Jason Knirck has argued, 'marked the key turning point in the relationship between gender and the Irish revolution'.

Gender aside, subsequent political developments also call into question the idea of a clear-cut Treaty divide: although several anti-Treaty TDs articulated anti-colonial or other radical perspectives, the Fianna Fáil party that later emerged from the anti-Treaty faction espoused the same socially conservative Catholic and cultural values as their opponents. Both sides articulated their opposing arguments in similar ways, drawing on a discourse of respectability that attributed an inferior social status and morality to their opponents.[27] Sharing the same goal—a territorially united, culturally Irish, separatist state—the movement was divided on strategy rather than principles, even if anti-Treaty rhetoric blurred the distinction between these.

Given the intimate and homogeneous nature of the republican movement, the emotional dynamics of the split bear close consideration. The most widely noted feature of the Treaty debates in the 'performative space' at Earlsfort Terrace,

Caoimhe Nic Dháibhéid has observed, was 'the tenor of the exchanges'. The deputies' expressions of love, hatred, betrayal, bitterness and sadness reinforced 'the emotional weight of their arguments'.[28] Concepts such as honour, loyalty, deceit, shame and hypocrisy were invoked as frequently as political ideals, while deputies wept at the conclusion of the debate.[29] Republican intellectuals such as Seán Ó Faoláin would later make sense of the conflict more in emotional than in political terms:

> The articles were duly put to the assembled Dail. There an orgy of word-combat between men and women who had once trusted one another like lovers but were now fast turning to mutual hatred and distrust at once began and went on for several weeks. It went on day after day. It was repeated night after night beside every fireside in the country. It was sealed in savage bitterness by the final ratification of the articles by a majority vote.[30]

The passions unleashed by the Treaty were not confined to Ireland. Across the 'Irish world', where the Irish revolution had produced an unprecedented surge of ethnic solidarity, the fallout of the Treaty (which was generally regarded more positively than at home) proved disorienting and demoralising. At Westminster, where the debates on the Treaty (as on Irish matters generally) were quickly forgotten, the Commons and Lords approved the settlement by large margins of 343 and 110 votes,[31] but the acrimonious tone of these debates, frequently characterised by colonial expressions of 'racial and civilizational superiority', demonstrated how British support for the Treaty resulted more from political expediency than from any acceptance of Ireland's right to self-determination.[32]

The case for the Treaty, a humiliating reversal of British policy, rested substantially on the need to recognise international realities. Churchill, for example, noted how Britain's interests in India, Egypt, the Dominions and the United States had been damaged 'by the loud insistent outcry raised by the Irish race all over the world'. Opponents of the settlement spoke of their bitterness, humiliation, shame and betrayal at the surrender of imperial and unionist interests. In a striking inversion of Irish anti-Treaty fears, British opponents of the Treaty predicted 'the disintegration of the Empire' and the emergence 'within a few years' of an Irish Republic. Ultimately, this key question of whether the Treaty would pave the way to independence or permanently subordinate Ireland to Empire—debated with urgency on both sides of the Irish Sea—would only be answered by future developments.

IV

On 7 January 1922 the Dáil ratified the Treaty by 64 votes to 57. When Arthur Griffith replaced de Valera as president by a margin of two votes, the anti-Treaty deputies acrimoniously departed the assembly. To what extent was the Civil War that began the following summer a product of this split?

A country where 'murder, rioting, martyrdom, and expulsion had all become common currency' by 1922 offered considerable potential for civil war, particularly given ongoing sectarian violence in Ulster and the power vacuum resulting from the gradual withdrawal of British forces from the South. In the 'grey area between the building of new states and the collapse of the old', Robert Lynch has noted, 'all kinds of fanatical paramilitaries, political radicals and armed idealists flourished'.[33] The collapse of republican unity resulting from the Treaty split further destabilised Ireland but it also diminished the potential for a more lethal sectarian civil war like that caused by Britain's partition of India.

Yet the fluidity of republican positions between Treaty and Civil War also suggested more benign scenarios. Rory O'Connor and Liam Lynch—who would lead the anti-Treaty IRA—initially indicated their willingness to work the Treaty, while two of the pro-Treaty military triumvirate, Michael Collins and Eoin O'Duffy, confided in comrades their willingness to break its terms.[34] Such malleability suggests that the Civil War was less an inevitable consequence of the Treaty split than a product of the political failure to surmount it. Two significant initiatives, a 'pact election' contested by both Sinn Féin factions and an effort to devise a sufficiently republican constitution to constrain anti-Treaty opposition within a constitutional framework, foundered during this period.

Much of the blame for this has been attributed to anti-Treaty republicans for repudiating popular support for the settlement—particularly de Valera, whose inflammatory rhetoric undermined efforts to seek compromise and extended political cover to IRA diehards—but, rather than arguing that the Irish people had no right to accept the Treaty, many anti-Treatyites insisted that they could only legitimately do so free from the threat of British coercion. The 1918 general election had, after all, produced a democratic mandate for the Irish Republic. In this interpretation, the conflict was one between the irreconcilable rights of national self-determination and majority rule, rather than between democrats and dictators.[35] While this may overlook the geopolitical realities limiting Irish sovereignty, it does bring into focus how the role of the British government—not least by frustrating Collins's efforts to seek compromise by demanding strict adherence to the terms of the Treaty—remains an underacknowledged factor in the slide towards civil war.

The Irish Civil War was an avoidable tragedy that had a devastating human, economic, psychological and political impact. In comparative terms, though, it was unremarkable: successions from empire were frequently followed by civil war, as new states struggled to assert legitimacy and control territory. Ireland's civil war was far less violent than that of a successor state such as Finland, which saw the death of 38,000 people (more than 1% of its total population of 3.2 million people), including 12,000 executions.[36] The comparable figures in Ireland were around 2,000 deaths and 81 executions. British power curtailed Irish sovereignty, but it also prevented the mass communal violence and forced population exchanges that accompanied post-war partitions in the collapsed German, Russian and Ottoman empires.

The Treaty, and the Civil War that it provoked, cast a long shadow. Indeed, its political legacy was more enduring than that resulting from more violent civil wars elsewhere. One significant consequence was a polarised two-party system that was not based on substantial ideological differences. As in Northern Ireland and other post-colonial entities, the continuing centrality of the national question frustrated the development of more progressive politics. In contrast, however, to the dangerous stasis in Ulster and the experience of most other successor states, the remarkable transition of power from Civil War victor to loser in 1932 enabled Irish democracy to flourish.

The divisiveness of the Treaty, and the absence of popular support for the connections to monarchy and empire that it enforced, made inevitable the progressive dismantling of the Irish Free State (replaced by Éire/Ireland in 1937 and proclaimed a republic in 1949). In a cruel twist of fate, it was de Valera who proved that Collins was right to argue that the Treaty would, in time, bring full independence, although Fianna Fáil's dominance ensured that this embarrassing truth was rarely acknowledged. As the political correspondent of the *Irish Times* observed when de Valera's government chose not to mark its 25th anniversary in 1946, 'the fact that the Oireachtas is able to assemble in Leinster House and direct the government of the country stems essentially from the Treaty'. Not much had changed by 1971, when Taoiseach Jack Lynch's refusal to commemorate the Treaty's 50th anniversary was denounced by the opposition as 'pigmy-minded pettiness'.[37]

A century on, the Treaty might now be considered to form part of Ireland's history rather than its politics. This is less evidently the case north of the border, the only place where the term 'Free Stater' is still in use, although it serves more as shorthand for Southern abandonment of Northern Catholics than as a critique of pro-Treaty politics. In the light of the post-Brexit re-emergence of tensions around the Irish border and growing uncertainty about the constitutional future of Northern Ireland, the most enduring of the Treaty's many flawed provisions turned out to be those relating to the Irish border and the relationship between the two Irish jurisdictions. Even on these most intractable of issues, however, important changes have taken place. Among the most significant consequences of the 1998 Good Friday/Belfast Agreement, which revisited with far greater imagination and sophistication the vexed questions of sovereignty and unity that so bedevilled the Treaty negotiations, is agreement that Ireland's future will be determined by those living on this island.

Endnotes

1 David Hogan [Frank Gallagher], *The four glorious years* (Dublin, 1953), p. 2.
2 Seán Ó Faoiláin, *Vive moi! An autobiography* (London, 1993 edn), p. 147.
3 Roy McLaren, *Empire and Ireland. The transatlantic career of the Canadian imperialist Hamar Greenwood, 1870–1948* (Montreal, 2015), p. 236.
4 Ernie O'Malley, *On another man's wound* (Cork, 2013 edn), pp 378–9.
5 Quoted in Diarmaid Ferriter, 'We must confront reality of our Civil War', *Irish Times*, 30 April 2021.
6 Quoted in Fearghal McGarry, 'Revolution, 1916–1923', in Thomas Bartlett (ed.), *The Cambridge History of Ireland*, vol. 4 (Cambridge, 2018), p. 287.
7 Dáil debates, 17 December 1921, Vol. T, No. 5.
8 Charles Townshend, *The Republic. The fight for Irish independence, 1918–1923* (London, 2013), pp 310–18.
9 *Ibid.*, p. 331.
10 Brian Maye, 'Negotiating the Treaty', *Irish Times*, 12 October 1996.
11 Diarmaid Ferriter, *A nation and not a rabble. The Irish revolution 1919–23* (London, 2015), p. 249.
12 Townshend, *The Republic*, p. 331.
13 Ferriter, *A nation and not a rabble*, pp 251–2.
14 Ronan Fanning, *Fatal path. British government and Irish revolution 1910–1922* (London, 2013), pp 278–9.
15 Ferriter, *A nation and not a rabble*, p. 250.
16 Fanning, *Fatal path*, p. 288. Quotes in the next two paragraphs derive from this source (pp 293–309).
17 Townshend, *The Republic*, p. 349.
18 Fanning, *Fatal path*, p. 310.
19 Townshend, *The Republic*, p. 341.
20 Heather Jones, 'Wars, dominions and monarchy: the transnational imperial context of Ireland's revolution, 1916–1922', in Patrick Mannion and Fearghal McGarry (eds), *A global history of Irish revolution* (New York, forthcoming).
21 Ó Faoiláin, *Vive moi*, p. 165; Ernie O'Malley, *The singing flame* (Dublin, 1978), p. 285.
22 Quoted in Roy Foster, 'Meditating in time of civil war', in Darragh Gannon and Fearghal McGarry (eds), *Ireland 1922. Independence, partition, civil war* (Dublin, 2021).
23 Townshend, *The Republic*, p. 449.
24 Jeffrey Prager, *Building democracy in Ireland* (Cambridge, 1986); J.J. Lee, *Ireland 1912–1985. Politics and society* (Cambridge, 1989), 67; Tom Garvin, *1922: the birth of Irish democracy* (Dublin, 1996).
25 Eunan O'Halpin and Mary Staines,'"Between two hells": the social, political and military backgrounds and motivations of the 121 TDs who voted for or against the Anglo-Irish Treaty in January 1922', in Liam Weeks and Mícheál Ó Fathartaigh (eds), *The Treaty. Debating and establishing the Irish state* (Dublin, 2018).
26 Jason Knirck, *Women of the Dáil. Gender, republicanism and the Anglo-Irish Treaty* (Dublin, 2006), pp 73–6. For criticism of this interpretation, see Claire McGing, 'Women's political representation in Dáil Éireann in revolutionary and post-revolutionary Ireland', in Linda Connolly (ed.), *Women and the Irish revolution* (Dublin, 2020), pp 88–92.
27 Gavin Foster, *The Irish Civil War and society. Politics, class, and conflict* (London, 2015).
28 Caoimhe Nic Dháibhéid, 'The politics of emotions', in Gannon and McGarry, *Ireland 1922*.
29 Jason Knirck, *Imagining Ireland's independence. The debates over the Anglo-Irish Treaty of 1921* (Lanham, MD, 2006), pp 175–6.
30 Ó Faoiláin, *Vive moi*, p. 148.
31 Townshend, *The Republic*, p. 234.
32 Seán Donnelly, 'Ireland in the imperial imagination: British nationalism and the Anglo-Irish Treaty', *Irish Studies Review* **27** (4) (2019), p. 495. Quotes in the next paragraph derive from the same source.
33 Robert Lynch, *The partition of Ireland 1918–1925* (Cambridge, 2019), pp 134–8.
34 Townshend, *The Republic*, pp 351–6.
35 Bill Kissane, *The politics of the Irish Civil War* (Oxford, 2005), pp 177–201.
36 Tuomas Tepora, 'Finnish Civil War 1918', *1914–1918 Online. International encyclopedia of the First World War* (https://encyclopedia.1914-1918-online.net/).
37 Diarmaid Ferriter, 'Birth of a nation: the Treaty that transformed Ireland', *Irish Times*, 3 December 2011.

Fig. 14: Sir John Lavery painting the portrait of David Lloyd George at the politician's home in Churt, Surrey, 6 November 1934.
Photograph by Reg Speller/Fox Photos/Getty Images

‘On neutral ground’: John Lavery’s Treaty portraits

Logan Sisley

Studio & State is possible thanks to the gift of an extraordinary group of paintings that John Lavery gave to the Municipal Gallery of Modern Art (now Hugh Lane Gallery) in 1935. The Lady Lavery Memorial Bequest comprised 34 paintings, including nine portraits of signatories to the 1921 Treaty between Great Britain and Ireland. Many of these portraits were realised during the Treaty negotiations in Lavery’s studio, a space that the artist envisaged as ‘neutral ground’. While exhibiting a certain wilful naivety, this idea enabled the Laverys’ London home to function as a meeting place for those of different political viewpoints. In the portraits Lavery presents the Irish and British signatories on a par, statesmen on equal terms, which is an extraordinary turn of events given that many of the Irish delegates had been imprisoned by the British authorities in the months and years preceding the Treaty negotiations.

The idea of recording in paint ‘both sides’ of a political question—in this case the opposing negotiating teams—is a recurring theme in Lavery’s work. It is evident in his gifts of two groups of paintings to the cities of Belfast and Dublin, and it mirrors the positions that John and Hazel Lavery negotiated in London and Dublin society. In 1919, Lavery gave the study for *The Royal Family at Buckingham Palace*, 1913 (National Portrait Gallery), to the Belfast Art Gallery (now the Ulster Museum). This donation followed his gift of an altarpiece to St Patrick's Catholic church in Belfast, where he had been baptised as a child. The dual donations were motivated because Lavery wanted 'to show the other side that I was not a bigot'.[1]

It was in 1916 that John Lavery's interest in painting Irish political subjects awakened, encouraged by Hazel, who believed that a series of Irish portraits might bring opposing sides together.[2] That year, he invited both the prominent unionist Edward Carson and the leader of the Irish Parliamentary Party, John Redmond, to sit for him. Lavery donated the two portraits to a charity sale and Ellen Duncan, the first curator of the Hugh Lane Gallery, sought a buyer to purchase them for the gallery. Lavery claimed that each of his subjects thought that the other's portrait was the better: 'Carson, knowing that I was a Catholic, although from Belfast, looking at the two portraits together, remarked, "Ah, it's easy to see which side you're on".'[3] Quips such as this would often follow the exhibition of Lavery's Irish portraits, as viewers attempted to read his political position from the paintings. These pairings set a precedent for Lavery's groups of paintings of the Anglo-Irish Treaty signatories and of the various 'contending elements' of his native city, Belfast.

Fig. 15: Sir John Lavery, *Sir Edward Carson, MP* (1916). Hugh Lane Gallery

Fig. 16: Sir John Lavery, *John E. Redmond, MP* (1916). Hugh Lane Gallery

While the Laverys made frequent visits to Ireland from 1914 onwards, they were firmly established in London society. John was born in Belfast but grew up in Scotland, where he was associated with a group of radical young painters known as the Glasgow Boys. He was commissioned to paint the State visit of Queen Victoria to the Glasgow International Exhibition in 1888, which launched his career as a society painter, and he moved to London soon after. He took up residence at 5 Cromwell Place, South Kensington, in 1899.

Fig. 17: Sir John Lavery, *The Artist's Studio: Lady Hazel Lavery with her Daughter Alice and Stepdaughter Eileen* (1910–13). National Gallery of Ireland

Cromwell Place became the Laverys' family home following their marriage in 1909. Shortly afterwards, John painted portraits of Hazel and Alice, marking the arrival of his new family. These include *Mother and Child* (1909), the first painting by Lavery of his five-year-old stepdaughter, and *The Artist's Studio: Lady Hazel Lavery with her Daughter Alice and Stepdaughter Eileen* (1910–13; National Gallery of Ireland).

While *Mother and Child* is an intimate portrait, *The Artist's Studio* is an ambitious, monumental canvas (measuring 344cm x 274cm) celebrating not only his family but also the painter's material, artistic and social status. It is similar in scale and composition to *The Royal Family at Buckingham Palace* and shows Hazel, Alice, Eileen and Aïda, the family's Moroccan maid. Lavery based the painting's composition and some prominent details, such as the placement of the dog, on Velázquez's *Las Meninas* (1656; Museo del Prado, Madrid). Other references are less literal, such as the artist's inclusion of himself, reflected in a mirror in the background, holding his palette and brush.

In Lavery's lofty studio, significant players from the cultural and political spheres mixed: the Prince of Wales, the Churchills, Eddie Marsh (Winston Churchill's private secretary), Michael Collins and the writer J.M. Barrie. Elizabeth, Countess of Fingall, recalled the gatherings there: '[Hazel's] house had come to be a centre of activity for a political group whose aim was real freedom for Ireland, by friendly treaty with England … She mixed her guests with gallant audacity. Michael Collins used to stay at Cromwell Place when he went over during the negotiations that preceded the Treaty … At her house he and Arthur Griffith met intimately men like Lord Birkenhead, Winston Churchill and Lord Londonderry, and were able to talk things over in a friendly way as they could have done nowhere else … Dinner was often in Sir John's studio upstairs, which made such a delightful background.'[4]

Amidst this lively environment, Lavery remained focused on securing sitters and completing paintings. Edward Knoblock recalled that Lavery seemed always to have a brush in hand, except for mealtimes, and quoted Cunninghame Graham's vivid description of Lavery's studio: 'The person who is being painted chats with her friends, doors close and open, a visitor has forgotten she left her husband sitting in a shop and screeches down the telephone … scents, noise, confusion … *Lavery sits painting on*. He answers everyone with a smile … not in the least regarding what they say … *and still the picture grows*.'[5]

Prior to the Treaty negotiations, Lavery sensed that 1921 was a pivotal year, the events of which should be recorded for posterity. On 11 July the Truce began, marking the end of the violence of the War of Independence. The next day Éamon de Valera, Arthur Griffith, Robert Barton, Austin Stack and Erskine Childers arrived in London for talks with the British government. So that John could paint their portraits, the Laverys cancelled summer plans to travel to Dublin, where the curator of the Gallery of Modern Art, Ellen Duncan, had offered John studio space.

Lavery painted Griffith and de Valera during this phase of negotiations in mid-1921. The pair were among a group that visited Lavery's studio on 16 July to view his paintings of the Most Revd Dr Mannix, the Appeal of Roger Casement and the funeral of Terence MacSwiney, so it may be that arrangements for sitting were made at that time. Later, during the Treaty negotiations, Erskine Childers wrote, 'Mr Griffith presumes that you will not require a sitting from him again'.[6] Griffith did, however, visit Lavery's studio the day he left London following the signing of the Treaty, so it is possible that sittings continued throughout 1921. It is—like much of Lavery's work—a sober portrait, in which it is hard to read the 'hysterical pride' that W.B. Yeats saw in his poem 'The Municipal Gallery Revisited' (1937).

De Valera is shown in profile, and his canvas is slightly larger than those of the Treaty signatories. Lavery recalled that he 'came to sit for a couple of hours. I was naturally more interested in what he looked like than in what he said—something to the effect that the mass of the people are like sheep in that they run after each other. I cannot remember what called forth the remark—the statement was not new to me. My regret is that I had so little time to paint him.'[7] His disavowal of an interest in politics is consistent with much of his writings on the subject. He was clearly astute in these matters but preferred to claim that his 'head was never really out of the paintpot'.[8]

Lavery exhibited his freshly painted portrait of de Valera at the Autumn Salon in Paris in November and December 1921, while the Treaty negotiations were under way. De Valera's 'severe austerity' contrasted with the room of contemporary Russian art that was also shown that year.[9] While comparing the sitter to a young missionary priest, *The Westminster Gazette* praised the painting, as it 'shows Sir John Lavery for once in a way thoroughly in sympathy with his sitter'.

The Dáil and Cabinet rejected the terms offered by David Lloyd George's government in August 1921, but correspondence between de Valera and Lloyd George continued. When relations reached a crisis point and Lloyd George hastily convened a Cabinet meeting in Inverness on 7 September, there was speculation that the Treaty negotiations might take place in the Scottish city. Lavery was prepared to travel to Inverness to document the event. He envisaged a group portrait commemorating the moment of signing, presumably on the lines of his other history paintings, such as *The End: The fore-cabin of "HMS Queen Elizabeth" with Admiral Beatty reading the terms of the surrender of the German Navy, Rosyth, 16th November 1918* (1918; Imperial War Museum). This proved impossible, so he opted for individual portraits during the Treaty negotiations that began in London in October 1921.

Éamon de Valera did not attend in person, but the Irish delegation including Arthur Griffith, Michael Collins, Robert Barton, Éamonn Duggan, George Gavan Duffy and Erskine Childers arrived on 8 and 9 October. Most of the delegation stayed at 22 Hans Place, while Collins stayed at 15 Cadogan Gardens; both addresses were just a short distance from the Laverys' home. Both Hazel and John Lavery reached out to the Irish delegates, as outlined in Sinéad McCoole's essay in this volume.

The close relationship between the Laverys, particularly Hazel, and Michael Collins is well documented. Lavery had previously intended to paint Collins on a visit to Ireland, against which Winston Churchill warned him. When Collins arrived for his sitting in the Cromwell Place studio during the Treaty negotiations, Lavery described him as 'a tall young Hercules with a pasty face, sparkling eyes, and a fascinating smile'. Lavery helped him take off a heavy overcoat, to which he clung, excusing himself by saying casually, 'There is a gun in the pocket'.

Fig. 18: Signed, limited edition print of John Lavery's 1921 portrait of Michael Collins, published by Wilson Hartnell.
Jackie Clarke Collection

Lavery described Collins as a patient sitter, 'but I noticed that he liked to sit facing the door. He was always on the alert.' In contrast, Collins wrote to Kitty Kiernan of his discomfort: 'By the way I sat today for my portrait—my interesting life! Absolute torture as I was expected to keep still and this, as you know, is a thing I cannot do.'[10] Another portraitist, Leo Whelan, declared Collins to be the worst sitter he ever had: 'He could not manage a moment's quiet. He was forever twisting and turning in the chair and was liable to dash from the studio without warning to attend to urgent business.'[11]

In June 1922 Lavery exhibited his 1921 portrait of Collins at the Grosvenor Galleries, London. One reviewer noted that the exhibition of the work 'shows that Mr. Collins has now become such a public personage that he has to be painted in more refinement and less embonpoint than he has in the flesh. One also notes that the catalogue adds "Esq." to Mike's name.'[12] The original portrait of Collins was given to Kitty Kiernan, and its whereabouts is today unknown. Ahead of his gift to the Hugh Lane Gallery in 1935, Lavery painted another portrait of Collins to hang alongside those of the other Treaty signatories.

The 1921 portrait survives through a print that was published by Wilson Hartnell & Co. along with a print of the portrait of Griffith. The portraits of the 'Founders of the Irish Free State' were advertised as 'national pictures', a term interrogated by Fintan Cullen in his essay in this volume. They were sold in an edition that included 175 copies signed by both the artist and the sitters. While the portrait in the Hugh Lane Gallery depicts the head and shoulders of Collins, the 1921 print shows him seated from the waist up with his hands clasped on his waist—and sporting a moustache. Collins was a wanted man and was known to have worn disguises, including false moustaches, to avoid detection. Maeve Sullivan, the daughter of Tim Healy, the first governor-general of the Irish Free State, recalled: 'I do not think that Sir John Lavery's portrait of him gives a true impression of him; it makes him look like a blacksmith, and to my mind he looked like a statue. However, Michael Collins (fortunately for him) had a face which lent itself to many disguises, and he may have been one of those people who keep one's interest by being different every time one sees them.'[13]

Lavery had seized the opportunity to get sittings with the Irish delegates while they were in London. While there is less archival material providing details of the sittings of Duffy, Duggan and Barton (the only subject in the group depicted reading), all the Irish delegates' portraits were completed by late November 1921.[14] The British delegates were another matter, but as they were in London they would have been more accessible. The Irish delegation first met the British team, comprising Lloyd George, Austen Chamberlain, Lord Birkenhead, Winston Churchill, Laming Worthington-Evans, Gordon Hewart and Hamar Greenwood, on 11 October. Worthington-Evans, Greenwood and Hewart were not key signatories and are absent from Lavery's Treaty portrait group. A portrait of Worthington-Evans was listed in correspondence in 1927, but was either never realised or simply not included in the gift to Dublin in 1935.

The portrait of David Lloyd George is dated 1922, though Lavery writes in his autobiography that he was not able to get a sitting with him until the mid-1930s, when the politician had settled in the English village of Churt, where he was 'the most amenable of sitters'. While Lavery did paint Lloyd George in 1935 (National Museum Wales), the Dublin portrait is consistent with those painted in the 1920s. It is a striking painting, with the sitter staring directly at the viewer. Lavery spoke fondly of Lloyd George in his autobiography. While again downplaying his interest in politics, he recalled that he had made friends with a number of statesmen: 'Amongst these I think Mr. Lloyd George has pride of place. Not because he settled the Irish Question (more or less), won the War, gave me a knighthood, and, it is said, "bitched the peace," but because of his great charm.'[15]

While Lavery's Treaty portraits follow a convention—the suited men sit against a dark background, with the white of their shirts and the light falling on their faces providing contrast—that of Lord Birkenhead, painted in 1923, stands out, as he appears in court rather than civilian dress. He is depicted wearing the levee dress coat worn by civil servants on formal occasions, with his army medals pinned to his chest. Lavery had previously painted Birkenhead in 1916, as he and George Gavan Duffy feature in his monumental picture of Roger Casement's appeal hearing. Birkenhead (then still F.E. Smith) was present as attorney general for England and Wales, while Gavan Duffy represented Casement. In meetings at Cromwell Place, Lavery recalled that Collins and Lord Birkenhead took to one another: 'Collins had a great admiration for the extraordinary facility of Birkenhead's address, and the un-English directness of his phraseology on occasion. No one could be as successfully insulting to "Noble Lords" as the "Galloper," … Many a morning before the Downing Street meetings Collins could be seen hurrying to meet Birkenhead. No one knows what took place.'[16]

Intriguingly, the portrait of Austen Chamberlain was left unfinished. While the face is fully realised, the torso and background are simply indicated by a few loose brushstrokes. The reason for this is unclear, as the Laverys and the Chamberlains mixed in the same social circles. In April 1922 John and Hazel assisted Mrs Austen Chamberlain in the arrangement of tableaux at the Court Theatre, to raise funds for the Children's County Hospital Fund. John even took on the role of the artist in Velázquez's *Las Meninas*, the very painting that he had referenced in *The Artist's Studio*.

Of the British delegates, the Laverys had the closest relationship with Winston Churchill. Indeed, the portrait of Churchill, painted in 1915, pre-dates the others in the Treaty collection by a number of years. John and Hazel enjoyed a close friendship with Winston and Clementine Churchill and their family. Clementine described John as having a 'very golden nature' and Hazel as 'very vivacious & amusing'.[17] The Laverys and the Churchills dined together regularly. Another regular guest at Cromwell Place, Duff Cooper, recorded on 22 January 1922 that 'We lunched with the Laverys … Hazel had had Winston and Michael Collins to dinner the night before and was very full of them and their delight with themselves at having come to an agreement with Craig.'[18]

The Laverys and the Churchills were in regular correspondence, and Hazel in particular corresponded with Winston on political matters. In 1922 she optimistically wrote that 'one assumes now that nothing can go wrong with the Treaty but one always trembles for the tragic fate that pursues Ireland'.[19] Winston Churchill was also a keen amateur artist and a painting companion of the Laverys. He painted John's studio in 1920 and wrote the foreword to the catalogue of John and Hazel's joint exhibition at the Alpine Club in London in 1921. John exhibited pictures of Morocco, the Riviera and other landscapes, while Hazel showed portrait and child studies, including the portrait of John that he gave to the Hugh Lane Gallery in 1935.

While Lavery settled for a series of portraits rather than a large canvas marking the moment the Treaty was signed, he did paint the passage of the legislation though the House of Lords in December 1921, resulting in *Viscount Morley Moving the Address*

Fig. 19: Sir John Lavery, *Viscount Morley Addressing the House of Lords,* (1921-22). Glasgow Museums

on the Irish Treaty in the House of Lords (1921–2; Glasgow Museums). He recalled that Lord Birkenhead and Sir Patrick Ford first suggested that he paint the two Houses of Parliament. Lavery was a friend and golfing companion of Patrick Ford, whom he had painted in 1908. Ford introduced Lavery to the sergeant-at-arms and he was allowed to take his portable 'pochade' paintbox into the Distinguished Visitors' enclosure.

He spent three days working in the chamber, one in studying the architecture with the members absent, and the others in sketching individual members. These oil sketches show the figures massed together in a manner reminiscent of a collage. In a study in the Fitzwilliam Museum, Cambridge, the distinctive profile of Edward Carson is easily identifiable alongside the figure of the Earl of Birkenhead in his gown and wig. As lord chancellor, Birkenhead sits on the Woolsack in the centre of the finished painting. Lavery is careful not to overlap the individual portraits, so that each figure is distinct. He had used this device before for large group scenes, such as at the pivotal point in his career when he painted Queen Victoria's visit to the International Exhibition in Glasgow in 1888, and his courtroom scene of Roger Casement's appeal in 1916.

Hazel, too, was present for the debates; she wrote to Michael Collins on 14 December 1921: 'Just come from House of Lords … where the Lord Chancellor replied with his usual devastating urbanity to the bitter but rather futile sarcasm of Carson. … The division was a very very close thing for the Government with a majority of one!!'[20]

Viscount Morley Moving the Address on the Irish Treaty in the House of Lords captures the moment when Viscount Morley replied to the king's speech, which put the Treaty to the House of Lords for ratification.[21] Lavery presents the view down on the scene from his position in the gallery, which is also captured in the study *The Ratification of the Irish Treaty in the English House of Lords, 1921* (National Gallery of Ireland). He would again use this symmetrical composition from an elevated viewpoint in his painting of the funeral Mass of Michael Collins at Dublin's pro-cathedral (1922; Hugh Lane Gallery).

Viscount Morley Moving the Address on the Irish Treaty in the House of Lords was exhibited at the Royal Academy in London and at the Royal Glasgow Institute of the Fine Arts in 1922. There was a debate over whether the painting should go to Glasgow or to the House of Lords. The Lords had first call on the picture. Glasgow was seen as the more democratic option, so it was purchased by the city where Lavery had begun his career as an artist.[22]

The context in which his paintings were shown was cleverly managed by Lavery. At the Royal Hibernian Academy, Dublin, he tended to show Irish subjects—Cardinal Logue, Archbishop Mannix, The Blessing of the Colours, Éamon de Valera, William Cosgrave and Kevin O'Higgins. At London's Royal Academy, to which Lavery was elected an Academician in 1921, he largely continued to show society portraits. The only Irish subjects shown in the early 1920s were Sir James Craig (1923; Ulster Museum), who in 1921 succeeded Edward Carson as leader of the Ulster Unionist Party and became the first prime minister of Northern Ireland, President Cosgrave (1923; Hugh Lane Gallery) and the Marquess of Londonderry. In 1922 he exhibited *The Royal Wedding Day, 28th February 1922* along with *Viscount Morley Moving the Address on the Irish Treaty in the House of Lords*. Two years later he exhibited *The Right Honourable J. Ramsay Macdonald Addressing the House of Commons*, an identical composition to his scene of the Lords. The 1924 RA show elicited disappointment from Philip Page in the *Daily Sketch*, who saw it as '… so *expected*, so cut and dried; in short, so dull. This is largely because the well-known names have been content to rely solely on the methods that made them well known … We know … that Sir John Lavery will be unimaginatively topical (this year it is a House of Commons scene) …'.[23]

While London audiences had fewer opportunities to see Lavery's Irish paintings, all of his Irish signatory portraits were shown in Paris in early 1922. Just weeks after the ratification of the Treaty by the Dáil, the Irish delegates were presented as statesmen on the international stage at the Exposition d'Art Irlandais at Galeries Barbazanges from 28 January to 25 February 1922, organised as part of the International Irish Race Congress. Lavery's inclusion was essential for the status

Fig. 20: Sir John Lavery, *Studies made in the House of Lords* (1921).
The Fitzwilliam Museum, Cambridge

of the exhibition, both for the loan of his own paintings and for his connections to others who might be persuaded to participate. Art O'Brien helped organise the exhibition and asked Lavery to lend his 'Pictures of modern Irish History'.[24] O'Brien, as London envoy of the first Dáil Éireann, had assisted with getting the delegates to sit for Lavery: 'I was very glad that eventually you were able to get the portraits of the five Delegates. At one time I thought I should hardly succeed in inducing them to make the necessary arrangements.'[25] Alongside the portraits of Griffith, Duggan, Duffy, Collins and Barton, the artist also lent his portrait of Cardinal Logue (1920), which would be included in his gift to Belfast in 1929, *Southwark Cathedral, London, 1920 (Terence MacSwiney)* (1920), and *Blessing of the Colours* (1922) (the preparatory versions in Crawford Art Gallery).

Lavery also showed his 1921 portrait of Michael Collins at the Grosvenor Gallery, a commercial gallery in London where he often exhibited. In June 1922 Collins visited the exhibition, where his likeness hung alongside *Hazel in Rose and Grey*. The latter painting was the subject of a controversy when the Tate Gallery refused to accept it as a gift from Lady Cunard. She resigned from the board of governors in protest and subsequently gave the painting to London's Guildhall Art Gallery. The paintings of Collins and Griffith (along with a portrait of Hazel) were exhibited at the Royal Scottish Academy, Edinburgh, in 1923, the year after the death of both men.

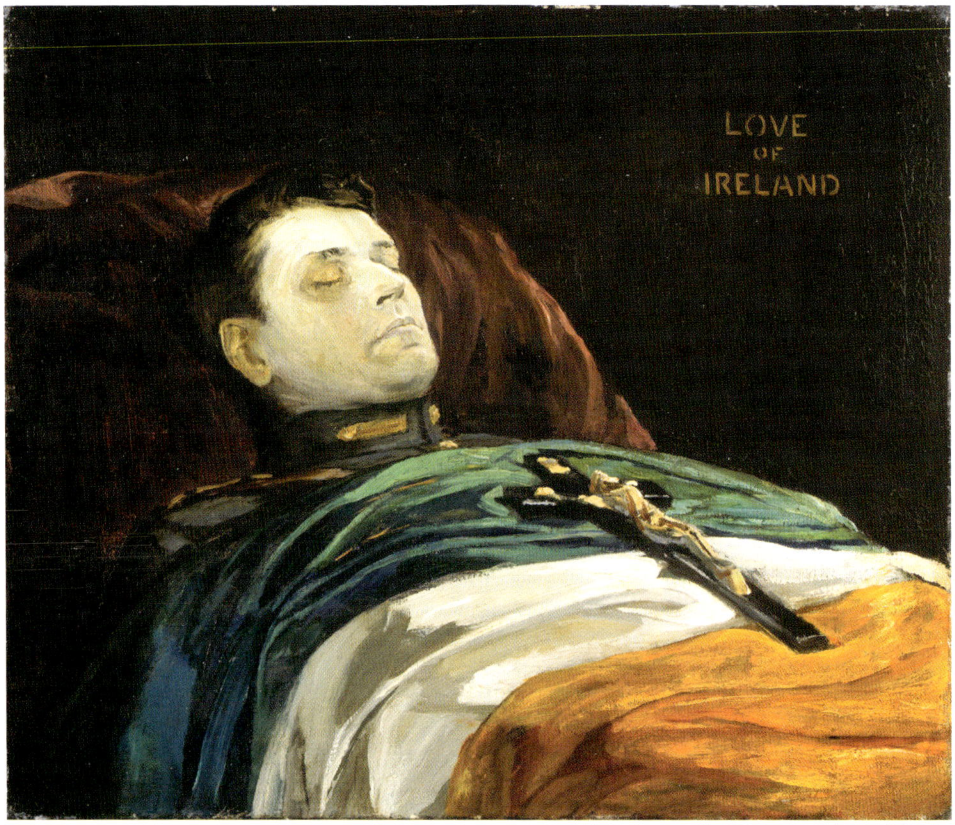

Fig. 21: Sir John Lavery, *Michael Collins (Love of Ireland)* (1922).
Hugh Lane Gallery

The Laverys travelled to Dublin after the shooting of Michael Collins, and John painted their dead friend in the chapel of St Vincent's Hospital before his body was taken to lie in state at City Hall. In *Michael Collins (Love of Ireland)* (1922; Hugh Lane Gallery) the pale figure of Collins is draped with the Irish tricolour; Lavery added the inscription 'Love of Ireland' at the last minute. The painting was finished back at the Cromwell Place studio, which Lavery opened to journalists in early September 1922, and was widely reproduced in the British press. It was sent to Paris to the Salon d'Automne, which opened on 1 November 1922, and it was reported that it would then go to Ireland as a gift to the nation.[26] While that would not happen until the following decade, the intent was there from the painting's inception. The group of paintings under discussion here were not a commission, nor were they for sale. Rather, Lavery kept them until he donated them to Dublin in 1935.

John and Hazel Lavery carefully managed the artist's career and legacy. His acute sense of equivalence in representation was expressed in a letter to Winston Churchill in 1923, ahead of a London exhibition in which Lavery had intended to show his Irish-themed pictures: 'Irish exhibition is off for the time being as I found I could not have the North adequately represented and I have had to switch off on to a landscape show'.[27] Despite having completed portraits of James Craig and Lord Carson, the balance was not correct in Lavery's eyes, and he exhibited landscapes instead.

Just as Lavery intended to give the portrait of Collins to Dublin, those of Craig and Carson were from the outset intended as a gift to the people of Belfast. They were among the 34 paintings that he gave to the Belfast Museum and Art Gallery (now the Ulster Museum) when it opened in 1929. The following year he was accorded the Freedom of the City of Belfast.

A similarly large donation, including the portraits of the Treaty signatories, would be made in time to Dublin. Lavery had been a supporter of Hugh Lane's efforts to found the Municipal Gallery of Modern Art (now the Hugh Lane Gallery) and proposed a large gift to the gallery as early as 1917. Following Lane's death in 1915, the curator Ellen Duncan sought gifts from artists in his memory. Lavery offered 'a Collection of Paintings and Bronzes representing a present day value of upwards of £35,000'.[28] While the gift did not eventuate at that time, Lavery pursued the idea of a gift to Dublin throughout the 1920s.

Lavery came close to giving the works directly to the State or to the National Gallery of Ireland (NGI), and the proposed gift was mediated by Thomas Bodkin, then director of the NGI. The subject-matter, however, did pose problems for the institution. Bodkin wrote to President Cosgrave that, while he supported the gift, 'I feel that it would not be proper to hang them all until a considerable time has elapsed. Many of them deal with events and persons who are the present cause of high and bitter controversial feelings. Some of them are portraits, which may prove in the future to merit inclusion in our gallery upon their artistic as against their historical interest. Others are portraits of living men who might object to their public and permanent display during their lifetime. A few of them would undoubtedly excite such feeling as might endanger their safety.'[29] The portrait of Lord Birkenhead in particular was cause for concern.

Lavery understood the sensitivities involved and gave Bodkin and Cosgrave discretion regarding the hanging arrangements. The gallery's policy of not showing the portraits of any living person offered a diplomatic solution. Later in 1927, Hazel wrote to Bodkin: 'John feels that it was perhaps a little premature, his offer, but that was my fault … John does not wish the gift to have any other than an <u>artistic</u> and <u>historical</u> significance, and to be <u>hung together</u> as <u>such</u> whenever the time is suitable.'[30] The foregrounding of artistic and historical merits over political concerns is consistent with John's writings on the matter, and was echoed by Cosgrave in his response: 'Sir John's munificent gift is of course above all party considerations. It is both artistic and historic.'[31]

The timing of the respective gifts to Belfast and Dublin was also a source of concern for the Free State government. The former was hastened by the completion of the Belfast Art Gallery and Museum, which opened in 1929, whereas in Dublin there was no suitable space to house them; Lavery specified a top-lit gallery. Hazel preferred an outright gift with no stipulations. Referring to Hugh Lane's contested bequest of a group of 39 paintings to the National Gallery, London, she wrote to Bodkin: 'Hugh Lane made enough complication for us all doing that, didn't he?'[32]

A solution to the question of a permanent home for the paintings arose as Dublin Corporation planned a new building for its Municipal Gallery of Modern Art at Charlemont House, which opened in 1933. There they could be hung together without restriction. Bodkin wrote to Commissioner Murphy from Dublin Corporation that the collection 'should add immeasurably to Dublin's prestige'.[33] The new gallery opened in 1933, with the top-lit galleries so desired by Lavery. Hazel passed away on New Year's Day 1935 and John donated 34 works in her honour as the Lady Lavery Memorial Bequest. The bequest included not only portraits of political figures but also images of cultural figures of the day—*George Bernard Shaw at Adelphi Terrace* (1927) and *Count John McCormack and his Family* (1929). A sensitive portrait of Alfred 'Andy' Cope (1925), assistant under-secretary for Ireland, 1920–2, was also included. Lavery wrote of him in his autobiography that 'There was one Englishman whose name seldom appeared in print, but who was working night and day behind the scenes to bring about a settlement'.[34]

The Lady Lavery Bequest paintings were exhibited in the gallery that had initially been left empty to house the disputed Lane Bequest pictures should they return to Dublin, which is evidence of the esteem the gift was accorded. John was consulted as to the display of the paintings. A bust of Hugh Lane by Albert Power had been the only artwork in the otherwise empty gallery and that was to remain, with portraits of Hazel and of the 'artist donor' by Hazel on either side. The five portraits of Irish Treaty signatories—Griffith, Collins, Duggan, Barton and Duffy—were grouped together, while Irish, British and Miscellaneous portraits formed other groups, as did Lavery's 'Subject' pictures, such as *Michael Collins (Love of Ireland)*, *Southwark Cathedral* and the *Court of Criminal Appeal*.

The gift echoes Hugh Lane's ethos in building a portrait collection for his proposed gallery in Dublin. The 'Series of Portraits of Contemporary Irishmen and Women' was a distinct component of Lane's vision for a Gallery of Modern Art. Lane not only purchased existing portraits but also commissioned works from John Butler Yeats and William Orpen and actively sought out public figures to sit for them. The sitters included those eminent in both political and cultural circles in Ireland, notably those associated with the Celtic Revival. They represented various positions on the political spectrum, or, as Thomas MacGreevy wrote, 'Dublin Corporation Irishmen as well as Dublin Castle Irishmen',[35] although, as Lucy McDiarmid has noted, they were 'mostly male and mostly Protestant, but not altogether',[36] consistent with power structures in Ireland at the time.

The Freedom of the City of Dublin was conferred on John Lavery at a reception at City Hall on 17 September 1935. In his speech he paid tribute to Hazel, who had encouraged him to do something for Ireland: 'I found it difficult because I was a portrait painter, and patriotism and paint are very difficult to amalgamate. I was naturally very anxious to be considered an Irishman, although in London, where I frequently had to tell them I was an Irishman, they said: "Oh yes, from Glasgow".'[37] Arguably, it was Lavery's complex personal history and identity that enabled him to navigate the social spheres of Glasgow, London and Dublin in order to first progress and then maintain his successful career over many decades. While he was at times self-effacing as regards politics, he clearly understood the role that images play in the construction of histories; he was a portrait painter to Britain's élite, after all. His position did leave him open to criticism in his own lifetime. Shortly after Lavery's death, Edward Knoblock wrote that the artist '... at times proved too much of a courtier to the detriment of his creative quality. He says so himself. "I have felt ashamed of having spent my life trying to please sitters and make friends instead of telling the truth and making enemies."'[38]

His Treaty portraits are among a group of works that fulfilled a desire in Lavery, conscious of his own legacy and reputation as an artist, to create something of significance. While the claim that 'the Irish Treaty was framed and almost signed at 5 Cromwell Place'[39] may be overstated, the Laverys played an important role in the process. Hazel may have been skilled at employing the studio as a site of encounter and debate, but for John it was foremost a place of work and securing the paintings was important to him, both in the moment and as a legacy.

Endnotes

1 John Lavery, *Life of a painter* (Boston, 1940), p. 217.
2 *Ibid.*, p. 208.
3 *Ibid.*, p. 217. See also Sinéad McCoole, *Passion and politics* (Dublin, 2010).
4 Elizabeth, Countess of Fingall, *Seventy years young* (Dublin, 1991), p. 402.
5 Edward Knoblock, 'Introduction', *Memorial exhibition of paintings by the late Sir John Lavery R.A.* (The Leicester Galleries, London, April 1941), p. 3.
6 Tate TGA 7245/220.
7 Lavery, *Life of a painter*, pp 222–3.
8 *Ibid.*, p. 223.
9 'de Valera's picture: Sir John Lavery exhibits it in Paris—a fine study', *Freeman's Journal*, 3 November 1921.
10 Michael Collins to Kitty Kiernan, 16 November 1921: León Ó Broin (ed.), *In great haste: the letters of Michael Collins and Kitty Kiernan* (Dublin, 1983), p. 58.
11 Quoted in Ó Broin (ed.), *In great haste*, p. 58.
12 'Grosvenor Galleries', *Sheffield Daily Telegraph*, Wednesday 21 June 1922, p. 6.
13 Extract from manuscript of a projected book by Mrs Tim Sullivan (Maeve Healy), daughter of Tim Healy and wife of ex-Chief Justice Tim Sullivan, loaned by her to the Director. 24th September, 1947. Chapter XIV. (Military Archives, WS0653.)
14 TS copy of letter from Art O'Brien to T. Hughes Kelly, 28 November 1921(National Library of Ireland MS 8,460/47).
15 Lavery, *Life of a painter*, p. 183.
16 *Ibid.*, p. 225.
17 Letter from CSC to WSC, on meeting with Sir John and Lady Lavery and Philip Kerr (later Lord Lothian) at Cap d'Ail, 21 February 1921 (Churchill Archive, University of Cambridge, CHAR 1/139/35-39).
18 Duff Cooper, *The Duff Cooper diaries 1915–1951*, edited by John Julius Norwich (London, 2005), p. 156. 'Craig' refers to Sir James Craig, the Ulster Unionist politician.
19 Letter from Sir John and Lady Lavery to WSC, on his illness [October 1922] (Churchill Archive, University of Cambridge, CHAR 1/157/73).
20 Letter from Lady Lavery to Michael Collins, 14 December 1921 (National Library of Ireland MS 31,712).
21 Hansard records this speech as taking place on 14 December, HL Deb. 14 December 1921, vol. 48, cc5–56.
22 See *Glasgow Herald*, Tuesday 24 October 1922.
23 Philip Page, 'Stodgy Academy pudding', *Daily Sketch*, 3 May 1924, p. 2.
24 Art O'Brien to John Lavery, 10 December 1921 (National Library of Ireland, MS 8,461/34). My thanks to Billy Shortall for his information on the Paris exhibition.
25 *Ibid.*
26 'London Letter', *Aberdeen Daily Journal*, 5 September 1922, p. 4.

27 Letter from Sir John Lavery to WSC, on the cancellation of his exhibition in Ireland, 15 January 1923 (Churchill Archives, University of Cambridge, CHAR 1/165/1).
28 TS copy of letter from John Lavery to Ellen Duncan, 28 June 1917 (Hugh Lane Gallery Archive).
29 TS Thomas Bodkin, NGI, to President Liam Cosgrave, 28 July 1927 (National Archives, TSCH/3/S5503).
30 MS extract from private letter addressed to the president by Lady Lavery, 28 December 1927 (National Archives, TSCH/3/S5503).
31 MS extract from president's reply to Lady Lavery, 6 January 1928 (National Archives, TSCH/3/S5503).
32 Copy of TS letter from Hazel Lavery to Thomas Bodkin, 31 August 1927 (National Archives).
33 Commissioner Murphy to Thomas Bodkin, 24 August 1929 (Hugh Lane Gallery Archive).
34 Lavery, *Life of a painter*, p. 233.
35 Thomas MacGreevy, 'Fifty years of Irish painting 1900–1950,' *The Capuchin Annual* (1949), pp 497–512.
36 Lucy McDiarmid, *The Irish art of controversy* (Ithaca, 2005), p. 18.
37 'Sir John Lavery's gift to Dublin', *The Irish Times*, 18 September 1935, p. 5.
38 Knoblock, 'Introduction', p. 6.
39 Countess of Fingall, *Seventy years young*, p. 402.

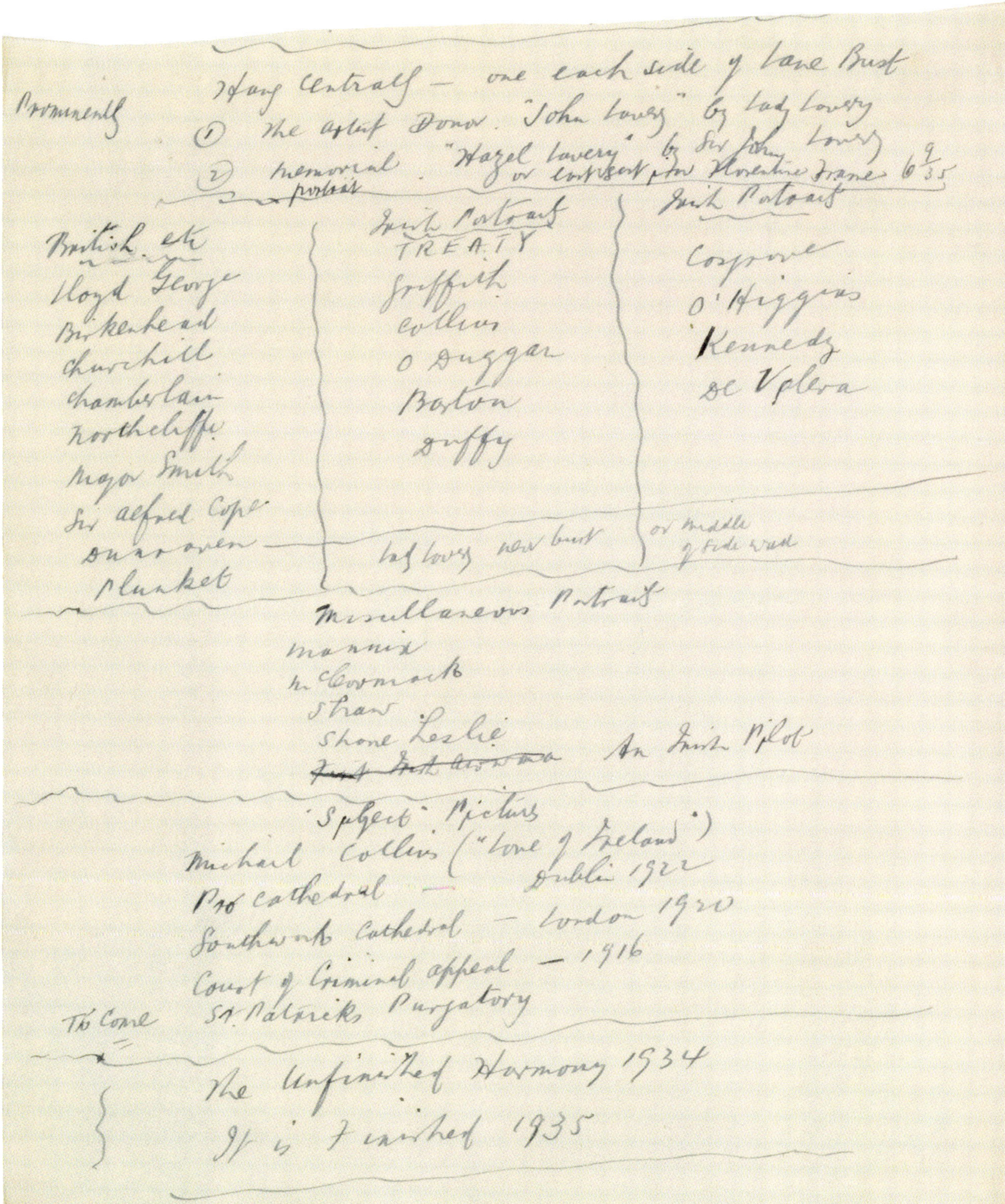

Hang Centrally — one each side of Lane Bust

Prominently
(1) The Artist Donor. "John Lavery" by Lady Lavery
(2) memorial portrait. "Hazel Lavery" by Sir John Lavery or [illegible] in Florentine frame 6 9/35

British etc
Lloyd George
Birkenhead
Churchill
Chamberlain
Northcliffe
Major Smith
Sir Alfred Cope
Dunraven
Plunket

Irish Portraits
TREATY
Griffith
Collins
O Duggan
Barton
Duffy
Lady Lavery new bust

Irish Portraits
Cosgrave
O'Higgins
Kennedy
de Valera
or middle of side wall

Miscellaneous Portraits
Mannix
McCormack
Shaw
Shane Leslie
~~[illegible]~~ An Irish Pilot

"Subject" Pictures
Michael Collins ("Love of Ireland")
Pro cathedral — Dublin 1922
Southwark Cathedral — London 1920
Court of Criminal appeal — 1916
To Come St. Patricks Purgatory

The Unfinished Harmony 1934
It is Finished 1935

Fig. 22: Notes on the hanging arrangements for the Lady Lavery Memorial Bequest through Sir John Lavery, 1935, by Hugh Lane Gallery curator John J. Reynolds.
Hugh Lane Gallery Archive

Fig. 23: National Portrait Gallery's 2000 commissioned work by John Wonnacott entitled *The Royal Family: A Centenary Portrait*
National Portrait Gallery, London

Sir John and Hazel, Lady Lavery — who really were the Knight and the Lady?

Exploring the importance of their home at 5 Cromwell Place, London, in 1921

Sinéad McCoole

In the year 2000 artist John Wonnacott was commissioned to paint *The Royal Family: A Centenary Portrait*, and central to the composition was Elizabeth, the Queen Mother. It was commissioned by the Trustees of the National Portrait Gallery to mark her 100th birthday, and it was also the first official portrait of the young princes William and Harry. Included in the family group was their father, Prince Charles, and their grandparents, Queen Elizabeth and Prince Philip. The composition was centred on figures in the centre of the White Drawing Room in Buckingham Palace. What is striking about the painting is the casual way in which the young Prince William is standing, and how he is dressed, in the splendid surroundings of the room. It seemed of its moment—a modern, contemporary depiction of the future king. This painting is not unique in its composition: it was deliberately based on an earlier painting of the royal family by Sir John Lavery (1856–1941). In a metaphorical sense, the Belfast-born painter had a hand in its creation.

In order to understand the role of Sir John Lavery and his wife, Hazel, Lady Lavery (1880–1935), in the events that led to the signing of the Articles of Agreement for a Treaty between the United Kingdom and Ireland, it is important to consider the unique position in London society occupied by this couple in the years leading up to 1921, the friendships that they forged, and their ability to move with ease in a number of circles while maintaining a popularity and a celebrity that seemed effortless. Although there is a vast archive,[1] much concerning the circumstances of the Laverys' access and influence was not documented. In this essay I will examine some of the small, almost imperceptible hints that remain to tell a wider story.

When King George V and Queen Mary arrived in Ireland on the royal yacht on 22 June 1921, the conflict later known as the War of Independence was ongoing. The streets of Belfast were lined with hundreds of people to greet them as their procession made its way to the City Hall, where the king officially opened the House of Commons of Northern Ireland. In his speech he appealed to all Irishmen to pause, 'to stretch out the hand of forbearance and conciliation, to forgive and forget, and to join in the making … a new era of peace, contentment and goodwill'. Two days later, on 24 June, Prime Minister David Lloyd George sent a letter to Éamon de Valera proposing a peace conference, in the hope that 'the King's appeal for reconciliation in Ireland shall not have been made in vain'.

A decade earlier, His Majesty had 'graciously permitted' William Hugh Spottiswoode of Eyre and Spottiswoode, Printers, and chairman of *The Sphere* and *The Tatler* to commission his friend John Lavery to paint a royal family portrait to 'present to the nation'. King George V and Queen Mary were painted alongside their son, the Prince of Wales (later King Edward VIII), and their daughter Mary, the Princess Royal (later the Countess of Harewood).[2] Another son, Albert (King George VI), was not included, as it was the decision of the king and queen to have only two of their five children in the painting.

This was not the first time that John Lavery had painted royalty: he had painted the king's grandmother in *The State Visit of Her Majesty, Queen Victoria to the International Exhibition Glasgow, 1888*. The creation of this historic work gave Lavery an understanding of access to influential sitters (and more clients), as he travelled all over England, Scotland and Europe painting individual sketches.[3]

For his royal family portrait the painter was given access to Buckingham Palace, as he described in his autobiography: 'my idea for the grouping and a sketch I made was pronounced satisfactory, so I was permitted to use the white drawing room as a studio'.[4] The king and queen were noted to have shown 'considerable interest'[5] in the work, [6] and Lavery had several individual sittings.[7] The Prince of Wales was less taken with the artist; he wrote in his diary that the two sessions lasting one and a half hours were 'an awful waste of time'.[8] Most unusually, the king and queen visited Lavery's studio in his home on two separate occasions, 9 March and 10 April 1913, to see the work in progress.

Lavery's home since 1898, 5 Cromwell Place, South Kensington, was the former residence of Sir Coutts Lindsay, the British watercolourist and founder of the Grosvenor Gallery. The studio occupied the whole top floor of the house. In early 1921 a second floor with bedrooms, bathrooms and dressing rooms was added.[9] The house was already well known to the public, as it had been photographed by *Vogue* for an article on 'notable women at home', as well as featuring in the *Lady's Pictorial*.

Fig. 24: Sir John Lavery, *The Royal Family* (1913).
National Portrait Gallery, London

The arrival of the king and queen at Lavery's studio attracted press attention; one newspaper reported:

> Now Mrs John Lavery is an American, and her child, who so nearly resembles her, has the same transatlantic simplicity and free easiness of manner which one finds so attractive.[10]

Meeting royalty 'was no strain' for Hazel.[11] Born in Chicago, from an early age Mrs Lavery was noted for her beauty, with striking red hair and brown eyes that led her parents to call her Hazel.[12] An aspiring artist, Hazel Martyn had come to Europe to study art and had met John Lavery in 1903 in the artist colony of Beg-Meil, France. They finally married in London in 1909.[13]

Fig. 25: Hazel, Lady Lavery (1880–1935).
Album / Alamy Stock Photo

In 1903 Lavery was 47 and had considerable standing in the international art world, with membership of the Royal Academy, the Hibernian Academy and the Royal Scottish Academy, as well as the Academies of Rome, Antwerp, Milan, Brussels and Stockholm. He had friendships with the leading artists of the day, as a founder member and vice-president of what became known as the International Society of Sculptors, Painters and Gravers.[14] He had been awarded honours such as the Cavaliere of the Crown of Italy and the Chevalier of the Order of Leopold in Belgium. In 1910 he exhibited 53 works at the 9th Venice Biennale and was subsequently requested by the Uffizi Gallery, Florence, to send a self-portrait for their permanent collection.

In the years since her arrival in London Mrs Lavery's fame had increased, along with her list of admirers. She featured regularly in the society magazines and in her husband's paintings, such as *La Femme* (1910)[15] and *The Silver Turban* (1911).[16] She was known as her husband's model first and foremost but also as a fashion

Fig. 26: Mr John Lavery painting *The Heroes of Loos* in the park, 23 August 1916.
Mauritius Images/TopFoto

trend-setter, and her celebrity was enhanced by the costumes she wore at the fancy-dress parties that were popular in the years before the Great War: the image of Hazel as Botticelli's figure of Spring at the London Picture Ball in 1914 was reproduced in European publications. She was a favourite model for the best-known London photographer, E.O. Hoppé, who photographed the 'who's who' of politics, art, literature and theatre. He had his studio in Room 33, Millais House, South Kensington, close to the Laverys' home.

During the First World War, 1914–18, Hazel was most identified as an American, as she joined with her fellow countrywomen to raise money for the war effort and entertained 'allied visitors and statesmen', according to Emerald Cunard (born Maud Alice Burke of San Francisco), wife of the grandson of the founder of the Cunard Shipping Line and one of London's best-known society hostesses.[17] The Anglo-American Yearbook noted John Lavery as one of 76 'distinguished Englishmen with American wives'.[18] As an American, Hazel's gatherings were seen to be outside the established political alliances, and the Laverys were known as neutral entertainers.[19]

Fig. 27: Interior of Sir John and Lady Lavery's home ('Her Ladyship's Sitting Room') by Bassano Ltd.
National Portrait Gallery, London

Extravagance was not essential for hostesses but imagination was important, according to Philip Zeigler in his study of Lady Diana Cooper.[20] Lady Diana later described Hazel as being a hostess who invited friends rather than entertaining in a 'tremendously big way'. She recalled Hazel as warmly welcoming, as if to say, 'When will you come to lunch or dinner?' 'Who would you like to meet?'[21] This was echoed by a journalist who described Hazel Lavery as hosting 'luncheons in her small dining room', where she held 'happy gatherings of distinguished men and women'.[22] The table sat eight and she never enlarged it.[23] Derek Patmore, the British writer and journalist, said that, like all great hostesses, she was 'interested in all kinds of people'. He later wrote that 'Famous beauties are apt to be strangely disappointing in private life; Madonna like beauties, when they open their mouths often betray themselves as fools'. He concluded, however, that Hazel Lavery was 'the exception to that rule'.[24] The archive that remains gives few glimpses of her intellect; the records from her own scrapbooks show her activities in society, including her appearance in David W. Griffith's patriotic film *A Great Love* (1918), in which she played a munitions worker.

In 1918 John Lavery was included in the Honours List and was knighted for his work as a war artist on the home front. The newly minted Sir John and Lady Lavery had managed to maintain their place in society despite several controversial decisions taken in the previous years by John Lavery on account of his nationality.

In 1916 Lavery approached Edward Carson and John Redmond to sit for him. These two politicians represented the Irish question of the day: Carson supported the Union of Great Britain and Ireland, while Redmond was working to establish 'Home Rule' for Ireland. The portraits were intended to raise money for the Irish War Hospital Supply Depot of the British Red Cross Society and the condition of their purchase was that they would be presented to the Municipal Gallery of Modern Art, Dublin. Many years later, Lavery wrote in his memoir: 'I went South and entered the political arena by inviting Edward Carson and John Redmond to sit on condition to a Dublin Gallery to hang side by side. Redmond only said plaintively "I have always had the idea that Carson and I might one day hang together. Now it has come to pass."'[25]

This was not Lavery's first entry into Irish politics: he had made a charitable donation to a sale organised by the National Aid Society at the Mansion House, Dublin, three weeks after the executions of the 1916 leaders for their part in the Easter Rising against the British Empire, which was engaged in the First World War at the time. He sold a blank canvas to support the families of those executed and imprisoned, with the offer that the person who purchased it would have his or her portrait painted. The identity of the purchaser remains unknown and the portrait has remained untraced.[26]

In 1916 Lavery also accepted a controversial commission from Mr Justice Darling to paint the appeal of Roger Casement, a former British diplomat, against a conviction for treason for his part in attempting to smuggle arms into Ireland for the Rising. He had previously painted Darling passing the death sentence, a painting called *The Black Cap*.[27] The acceptance of this commission was highly controversial, as one newspaper commentator noted:

> Girls in white, girls on the sand in full sun or girls on horseback—such used to be Lavery's themes. But the penalty of fame has brought him other subjects including a Coronation and a trial. Of all the trials not to paint, the Casement trial, I should have thought, would have had first place.[28]

It was distasteful to many that he was painting the trial of a man whose death was a foregone conclusion; moreover, diaries that purported to detail Casement's homosexuality were circulating in London.[29] Lavery's methodology of meeting each person to prepare a likeness meant that he came into contact with Casement's legal team and supporters. He contacted George Gavan Duffy, Casement's lawyer and later one of the signatories of the Anglo-Irish Treaty. The reply came from

Gavan Duffy's wife, Margaret, who supplied information on the women featured in the painting: Margaret herself, Miss Ada McNeill and Gertrude Parry, Casement's cousin. Lavery also looked for information on the lady in the gallery, Eva Gore Booth, but in the end he did not meet her and he did not include the gallery in the final painting.[30]

In the subsequent years the Laverys followed events in Ireland at a remove, through the newspapers. In March 1920, Lavery later recalled, 'Things were getting pretty bad [...] when an invitation came to Hazel' to meet the new prime minister, David Lloyd George, at Sir Philip Sassoon's. Sassoon was Lloyd George's parliamentary private secretary. According to Lavery's account, he encouraged his wife to go and meet him, telling her: 'Now is your chance to do something for Ireland'. On her return, Hazel reported that the 'Welsh Wizard', when they met, had shifted the focus away from the Irish question. She thought that he was charming and that he would show sympathy to Ireland, but when she read newspaper accounts of the Black and Tans and their actions she was very disappointed.[31] Lavery's description of his wife gives the impression that she had no understanding of the situation in Ireland; elsewhere in his memoir he remarks that she had a 'dreamy romantic view' of Ireland and that her Ireland was 'as unreal as a mirage in the desert'.[32]

In October 1920, during what became known as 'the year of terror', the Laverys were in Ireland, as John was painting portraits of the Catholic and Protestant religious leaders. In time these works would form a collection for his native Belfast. Later that year the Government of Ireland Act, 1920, legislated for two parliaments. During this visit the Laverys met with people from all sides: they lunched with the Unionist lord mayor of Belfast and attended a royal reception in the city before travelling to have a portrait sitting with Cardinal Michael Logue, who organised a reception for them with key people from the Catholic community in Armagh.

They also undertook a motoring tour, covering 150 miles a day,[33] and spent some time in Connemara on the west coast. John's story was that they were searching for Michael Collins, as Hazel hoped to locate him for his portrait. In his autobiography Lavery claimed that Winston Churchill had warned him about this plan: 'Be careful, my dear John, our men are not all good shots'.[34] Lavery wrote from Ireland to Churchill, who was then secretary of state for war and had asked Lavery for his opinion of the situation there.[35] The letter, reproduced in *Life of a painter,* opens with Lavery writing that he had not previously had the courage to tell Churchill what he thought but that he had now decided to state his beliefs (with the encouragement of his wife, as the letter is signed by both Hazel and John).

> The Prime Minister has said he is prepared for a million casualties and five years of war. I believe ten million- and fifty-years' war will not bring about the result desired. I believe that the removal of the Castle[36] and all its works, leaving Irishmen to settle their own affairs is the only solution left.[37]

Lavery continued to document events as they unfolded in Irish politics. In *Southwark Cathedral* he depicted the Requiem Mass held in October 1920 for Terence MacSwiney, lord mayor of Cork, who had died on hunger strike in Brixton Prison after 74 days of protesting his status as a prisoner of war. Thousands attended the memorial service, which generated strong sympathy for Irish independence. Once again Sir John Lavery placed himself in the centre of Irish affairs, putting himself in a public setting to record the event. Later he painted a portrait of MacSwiney's young widow, Muriel, who was then in the United States following her husband's death, giving testimony to the American Commission for Conditions in Ireland.[38]

In his autobiography Lavery gives Hazel the credit for his involvement with Ireland. 'When Hazel asked me to do something for my country, I replied "I cannot see that I can do anything without mixing myself with religion or politics and I have no time to differ with people". "Don't differ", was her reply, "agree with them all as you do anyway".'[39] This, he says, sparked the idea that they might make the 'studio neutral ground where both sides could meet'.[40] On 11 July 1921 a truce came into force. The Laverys adjusted their summer plans. In a letter to Ellen Duncan, Curator of the Municipal Gallery of Modern Art in Dublin, on 14 July, Lavery said that 'The presence of the Sinn Féin Leaders in London has somewhat altered my plans and it may now be the autumn before I can get to Ireland'.

In the years that followed, even when he undertook subject-matter that may have been deemed controversial, Sir John Lavery did not lose royal patronage.[41] In 1921 Princess Marie Louise began commissioning a special project for Queen Mary. Sir John was engaged to paint two more royal portraits, the miniatures of Queen Alexandra (RCIN 408539) and King Edward VII (RCIN 408538), to be hung in the saloon of Queen Mary's dolls' house at Windsor.[42]

On 16 July 1921 Éamon de Valera, Arthur Griffith, Count Plunkett and Sir Shane Leslie dined with the Laverys. It is recorded in Leslie's diary that other members of the delegation attended but they are not mentioned by name.[43] Sir Shane Leslie was a long-standing admirer of Hazel Lavery—indeed, his wife in response set up a 'husband protection society'. He later reflected that he was used simply 'as a messenger betwixt gods'.[44] His connections included the Catholic hierarchy, Anglo-Irish families and his cousin Winston Churchill. His diary entry describes his impression of the delegation as being 'as nervous and reticent as though gunmen were watching them'.[45] Lavery had completed the portraits of Éamon de Valera and Arthur Griffith by the time the delegation was preparing to return to Dublin. The proposals they had negotiated received no support, and the terms were officially rejected on 10 August. Shane Leslie wrote to Hazel Lavery on 20 August, saying that he was eager to discuss the events of the previous ten days and would give anything to talk it over in the Lavery studio, and enquiring as to Sir John's thoughts on the matter.[46]

When the Laverys were in Dublin they visited what Hazel described as 'Government Buildings'. They met Desmond FitzGerald, director of publicity, so it is most likely that they visited 6 Harcourt Street.[47] It is unclear what the Laverys were doing during this visit, but Sir Shane Leslie wrote to Hazel: 'You have been a dear friend to Ireland, and I kiss your feet'. On their return to London, Lady Lavery notes a meeting in Cromwell Place on 10 September 1921 in her scrapbook. There is no reference to who attended or its subject-matter, but it relates to political meetings about Ireland.[48] Alfred Cope[49] may have been one of those who attended; as a member of the British administration he had been liaising with Sinn Féin. He had known the Laverys for years and at this time described how he was 'rushed over to their home'.[50] Another possible attendee was Arthur Rose Vincent CBE, who had been a member of the judicial service in Mombassa, China and Zanzibar and the British representative in Chicago from 1917 to 1919. He then returned to Ireland and was living in Muckross House, Killarney, Co. Kerry, which was owned by his parents-in-law, and at this time became another secret emissary between both sides.[51]

The timing of this meeting is highly significant, as it coincides with the meeting of the British Cabinet in Inverness, where the Irish question was being discussed. It was the original intention that negotiations would begin in Inverness on 20 September 1921. At this time John Lavery was in correspondence with Art O'Brien of the Irish Self-Determination League. Newspaper reports suggested that the conference was to take place in Inverness, so Lavery sought permission to 'make a pictorial record of the meeting there'. He envisaged a large history painting 'on the scale of the Casement picture' against 'the picturesque background of Inverness'. He also requested permission and co-operation from O'Brien to paint portraits of the Irish Treaty delegates, as he had previously done with de Valera and Griffith. He wanted to paint another portrait of de Valera; he felt that an existing portrait was 'fairly good' but he believed that he 'could do him more justice'. O'Brien agreed to help arrange another de Valera sitting, if he did return, while also commenting that 'the first portrait is splendid'.[52]

Lady Lavery notes another meeting on 1 October 1921. The date may again be significant, as it is the day after a decision was taken in Dublin to send the plenipotentiaries to London. A new invitation had been issued to ascertain how the 'association of Ireland with the community of nations known as the British Empire may be best reconciled with Irish national aspirations'. Arthur Griffith now headed the delegation, consisting of Michael Collins, Éamonn Duggan, George Gavan Duffy and Robert Barton, with Erskine Childers and Finian Lynch as secretaries and Desmond FitzGerald as chief of the Publicity Department. Also travelling were female secretaries and clerks.[53] Éamon de Valera, however, remained in Ireland.

Hazel immediately wrote to Arthur Griffith asking him to come to luncheon or dinner, although she did 'realize how very engaged' he would be during his time in London. She asked him to come the following Saturday night: 'we can dine at any hour that suits you'. She suggested bringing Mr Kennedy (the attorney general) and it is clear from the letter that she had already met him. She acknowledges that she knows that Mr Collins was travelling over later,[54] and adds 'but of course you will extend the invitation to him if he comes after all'.[55]

On 6 October John Lavery also requested three hours of the delegates' individual time to paint their portraits. He wrote: 'I expect every minute of your time is taken up, but merely telephone the day before and I shall be at the disposition of the sitter'.[56]

On 11 October the Irish political representatives met the British delegation, consisting of David Lloyd George, Austen Chamberlain, Lord Birkenhead, Winston Churchill,[57] Sir Laming Worthington-Evans, Sir Gordon Hewart and Sir Hamar Greenwood, for the first time. Shane Leslie recalled meeting Prime Minister David Lloyd George at Philip Sassoon's[58] in Park Lane the day after the peace negotiations began. He was introduced by Hazel and spoke to the prime minister for half an hour about Michael Collins and a possible Tory revolt.[59] In his memoir *The long shadows*, published in 1966, he plays down this event. In his description, Hazel summoned him to Sir Philip Sassoon's and for him the 'climax' of the night was the prime minister listening to him for half an hour on his 'immediate plan for settling the Irish question'.[60]

On 12 October Erskine Childers replied to Sir John Lavery on behalf of the delegates: 'will gladly arrange for a sitting as soon as it becomes possible to fix any dates. At the present the time is too full to arrange anything.'[61] On 21 October Hazel wrote to Desmond FitzGerald, chief of the Publicity Department for Sinn Féin (the envelope was addressed to him at the Publicity Department, Irish Delegation of Plenipotentiaries, London);[62] she notes her disappointment that he had not come to see her 'in spite of all our mutual friends and interest'.[63] During the month of October Sir John completed the portraits of Éamonn J. Duggan, Robert Barton and George Gavan Duffy. Hazel also wrote to Michael Collins at his sister's address—Hannie Collins lived in South Kensington and worked for the Post Office Savings Bank as a clerk—but she received no reply.[64]

That October the Laverys launched their joint exhibition at the Alpine Club Galleries and invited the Irish delegation to the private viewing. *The Sketch* reported that it was the 'smartest private view imaginable … filled with the best-known society people'.[65] Hazel, then in her early 40s (although claiming to be six years younger than she actually was),[66] had continued with her art, signing her work as 'Hazell', making etchings and producing works in charcoal and chalk.[67]

Winston Churchill launched the exhibition and wrote the foreword to the catalogue. The Churchills were the Laverys' neighbours, living in 41 Cromwell Place. John Lavery and Winston Churchill painted together. It was Hazel who had given Churchill informal painting lessons, according to John Colville: 'Women with achievements in their own right seldom crossed Churchill's path or impressed him when they did, they were exceptions; when Hazel Lavery spent hours teaching him to paint he was grateful for that'. [68] In his opening speech at the exhibition Churchill

Sir John and Lady Lavery at the Exhibition of their Pictures at the Alpine Club Galleries

Lady Lavery, the wife of the distinguished artist, is holding an exhibition of her own work, in company with that of her husband, in the galleries of the Alpine Club. She is responsible for a number of paintings and drawings which go to show that she has real artistic ability and a clever mastery of technique. Mr. Winston Churchill has written the preface to her catalogue. In the above picture Lady Lavery is seen superintending the hanging of her pictures, whilst Sir John is busy varnishing one of the canvases

Fig. 28: Sir John and Lady Lavery at Alpine Club Galleries.
© Illustrated London News Ltd/Mary Evans

THE BEST ATTENDED PRIVATE VIEW: SOCIETY AND SIR JOHN AND LADY LAVERY'S PICTURES.

LADY GLENCONNER.

LORD LATHOM AND MRS. SOMERSET MAUGHAM.

MRS. R. GUINNESS AND HER DAUGHTER

THE DUKE AND DUCHESS OF ABERCORN.

MRS. JOWETT AND MRS. DENNIS EADIE.

MRS. LIONEL GUEST.

COLONEL JAMES FORBES AND MRS. FORBES TALKING TO SIR VICTOR AND LADY WARRENDER.

MR. GARDNER, LADY CURZON, AND MRS. RALPH PETO.

MRS. CYRIL ASQUITH, LADY POLLOCK, AND MISS ELIZABETH POLLOCK.

THE SPANISH AMBASSADOR AND MME. MERRY DEL VAL.

The show of pictures by Sir John and Lady Lavery at the Alpine Galleries was certainly the smartest private view imaginable. On the two days—the Saturday and Sunday—the place was filled with all the best known Society people, a number of whom had come to see their own portraits, most skilfully painted by Lady Lavery. It is not often that husband and wife both gain such distinction in the same art as is the case with Sir John and Lady Lavery.

Fig. 29: 'The best attended private view': Lavery exhibition, 1921.
© Illustrated London News Ltd/Mary Evans

said of Hazel's work: 'There is an unquestionably steady current of persistent brain work, conscious or unconscious behind the pictures, which she allows us to see'.[69] In his foreword to the catalogue his praise for Hazel's work was rather overblown: 'But there is already a change: the woman painter of surpassing genius has yet to appear, but there must be at least a dozen women working today whose pictures would command attention in any contemporary show. Of these Lady Lavery is surely one …'.[70]

In mid-November Michael Collins arrived unannounced at the Laverys' South Kensington home, and Sir John seems to have believed that it was the letter to Hannie Collins that had brought about the portrait sitting.[71] On 16 November Collins wrote to his fiancée Kitty Kiernan that he found it 'absolute torture' to sit. He said that if he got a picture of the portrait he would send one.[72] During the month of November the negotiations were under way; after the initial sessions, the delegations had divided up into sub-conferences, with direct negotiations undertaken with Griffith and Collins. The delegation dined several times at the Laverys'. Among those who attended was one of Hazel's oldest friends in London,[73]Eddie Marsh, Churchill's private secretary. At first, according to Marsh, Churchill told him that he was beguiled by mixing with the Irish delegation.[74] The company also included the author J.M. Barrie, best known for his work *Peter Pan*, who struck up a friendship with Collins. Hazel described Barrie as 'such a help' and she defended the Irish delegation against their mutual friends, including the Londonderrys.[75] One member of the British delegation, F.E. Smith (Lord Birkenhead), a close friend of the Laverys, also attended their luncheons at this time.[76] According to Frank Pakenham, these informal meetings fostered an unlikely friendship between Collins and Smith. Chamberlain believed that agreement with the Irish would never have been achieved without this informal contact.[77]

Fig. 30: Interior of Sir John and Lady Lavery's home ('The Dining Room') by Bassano Ltd.
National Portrait Gallery, London

By 1 December the British had handed over their final proposals: dominion status for Ireland (similar to that of Canada), the use of the title 'Irish Free State' and an oath of allegiance. These terms were brought back to Dublin. Changes to the document were presented by Robert Barton and George Gavan Duffy. The talks broke down, and Prime Minister David Lloyd George, aware of Arthur Griffith's willingness to compromise, moved to win Collins over. On 4 December Griffith was urged to get Collins to meet with Lloyd George alone—that very night, according to several accounts.[78] Hazel urged Collins to agree and even travelled with him to Downing Street, wearing her favourite opera coat.[79] The following day Michael Collins announced his intention to sign. Erskine Childers wrote to his wife: 'Everything changed at the last moment. This placed the minority in a frightful position—a cruel position. Nevertheless B. [Bob, his cousin Robert Barton] held out until the last moment. Then he weakened, overcome by M.C. [Michael Collins] I think.'[80] That same day Childers wrote in his diary: 'John Lavery asked to paint my portrait; refused'.[81]

In 1948 D.B. Wyndham Lewis, writing in *The Tatler*, claimed that 5 Cromwell Place was for a time 'the most important house in the British Empire': as the 'conflict looked like resolving into another bloodbath', the leaders from both sides found a place to talk.[82] Oliver St John Gogarty wrote: 'The Laverys did more to bring about a settlement than all the weary official and overlooked weeks at Hans Place'.[83]

When Hazel died in January 1935 her friendship with Michael Collins featured in some of the obituaries. The *Larne Times* and the *Belfast Telegraph* both reported: 'a great friend of Michael Collins … once during the negotiations she accompanied Michael Collins to Downing Street'.[84] The *United Ireland* newspaper stated: 'Few people did more than[85] Lady Lavery to stimulate feeling in authoritative quarters in Great Britain against murder and outrages which were being perpetrated by the British forces here prior to the Truce'.[86]

In contrast, in private correspondence Moya Llewelyn Davies, who with her husband Crompton (a British civil servant) had been central to advising[87] Michael Collins during the Treaty negotiations, wrote of the Laverys to Private Secretary Diarmuid O'Hegarty: 'I felt that both the Laverys were publicity hunters, running after the men of the moment, the one to paint, the other to embrace'.[88] A decade earlier, Moya Llewelyn Davies had written to Josephine McNeill[89] of Lady Lavery's claims to have made the Treaty: 'I have heard this claim of Lady Lavery's before and of her supplying the material for a novel in which she appears as the heroine of the liberation of Ireland with Mick as the hero …'.[90]

Lady Lavery kept up her friendship with Hannie Collins after her brother's death and continued to invite her to fashionable parties in the decade that followed the Treaty negotiations.[91] When Hannie Collins was asked for an assessment of Lady Lavery fifteen years after her death, she wrote: 'an exceptional character in every way—in addition to her beauty and kindness and charm of character she was extremely well endowed mentally—a thing she generally managed to conceal. I loved her and shall always regret her loss.'[92]

Fig. 31: Michael Collins by Lady Lavery.

In his own lifetime Sir John Lavery presented 63 paintings to two cities in Ireland, his native Belfast and Dublin. In 1929 the newly opened Belfast Museum (now the Ulster Museum) was delighted to accept a gift from one of their own. His planned gift to the National Gallery of Ireland in Dublin could not be accepted, as it contained images of living people. The collection was finally presented to the Municipal Gallery of Modern Art (now the Hugh Lane Gallery) in memory of Hazel, Lady Lavery in 1935.

Endnotes

1 For additional information please see 'The Laverys and their role in the emergence of the Irish state' (unpublished MA thesis, University College Dublin, 1991); *Hazel: a life of Lady Lavery, 1880–1935* (Dublin, 1996; reissued with new content in 2016); *The salon revisited*, catalogue to accompany the Hugh Lane Gallery's *Passion and Politics* exhibition (2010); 'Courting controversy: John Lavery and the Court of Criminal Appeal', in *High Treason: Roger Casement*, catalogue accompanying the exhibition of the same name at the Hugh Lane Gallery (2016).

2 Sir John Lavery painted the princess royal's wedding procession in Green Park in 1922.

3 This painting is in the collection of Culture and Sport Glasgow (Museums).

4 John Lavery, *The life of a painter* (Boston, 1940), p. 159. Lavery retained one of the sketches, which he presented to the Ulster Museum in 1919 at the same time as he presented *The Madonna of the Lakes* to St Patrick's Church, as he wanted the two gifts to be in the newspapers at the same time (information contained in letters to the parish priest of St Patrick's Church,

Belfast, in the possession of the parish when consulted by the author in 2010).

5 Royal Collection Trust, Catalogue Entry RCIN 407134.

6 In 1913 the artist presented Queen Mary with the preparatory sketches of her image and those of the two children (Royal Collection Trust, Catalogue Entries, dated 1913: Queen Mary, RCIN 407141; Edward VII, RCIN 407133; Mary, Princess Royal, RCIN 407132). The portrait of King George (RCIN 407142) was presented in 1918 following its exhibition at the RSA in 1914 and in the RA in 1918. Another version of a study of George V was sold at Sotheby's in New York on 24 October 2006.

7 The king's sittings: 20, 23 and 25 February, and 4 and 13 April 1913.

8 Royal Collection Trust, Catalogue Entry RCIN 407133.

9 https://www.rbkc.gov.uk

10 'News and Views: The King and Mr John Lavery's Little Girl': undated press cutting, Lady Lavery scrapbooks (private collection).

11 Lavery, *Life of a painter*, p. 195.

12 Her birth certificate, dated 14 March 1880, bears no name. Three months later in the Census she is named Elsa, but this is the only mention of that name in documentation; elsewhere her name is given as Hazel.

13 Alice Martyn, Hazel's widowed mother, did not encourage the romance between her 23-year-old daughter and the 47-year-old Irish artist. For the full account of this courtship see Sinéad McCoole, *Hazel: a life of Lady Lavery* (Dublin, 1996).

14 He resigned as vice-president in November 1903.

15 It was called *Ma Femme* when it was exhibited at the Paris Salon. It was also called *Portrait of the Artist's Wife* and *Mrs Lavery Sketching*, 1910.

16 Exhibition in the Royal Academy, 1912. This painting can be seen in the drawing room of the Laverys' home in the *Lady's Pictorial* of 13 December 1919. It was later sold into a private collection.

17 Sir Shane Leslie to Lady Audrey Morris, 15 June 1950 (Shane Leslie Collection, Georgetown University, Washington DC), quoted in Sinéad McCoole, 'Lady Lavery, her salon and its role in the emergence of the Irish Free State' (unpublished MA thesis, University College Dublin, 1991).

18 Undated press cutting, Lady Lavery scrapbooks (private collection).

19 Lady Audrey Morris, unpublished biography of Lady Lavery (author's collection).

20 Philip Zeigler, *Diana Cooper* (London, 1983), pp 193–4.

21 Elizabeth, Countess of Fingall, *Seventy years young* (New York, 1937), p. 402.

22 Undated press cutting, Lady Lavery scrapbooks (private collection).

23 Lady Audrey Morris, unpublished biography of Lady Lavery.

24 Derek Patmore, 'Who's who', in *Woman's Life*, 16 May 1931.

25 Lavery, *Life of a painter*, p. 208. The paintings were purchased in June 1917 by Sir W. Hutcheson Poe for £500 and presented to the Municipal Gallery of Modern Art.

26 *United Ireland*, 12 January 1935, states that the item was purchased for £800.

27 *The Black Cap, Portrait of Lord Darling*, 1905. Collection the Honourable Society of the Inner Temple, London.

28 Undated press cutting, Lady Lavery scrapbooks (private collection), quoted in 'Courting controversy: John Lavery and the Court of Criminal Appeal', in *High Treason: Roger Casement* (Dublin, 2016).

29 The so-called 'Black Diaries' were circulated to various influential people to counteract sympathy for Casement. They were forgeries. See Angus Mitchell, *The Amazon Journal of Roger Casement* (Dublin, 1997).

30 This figure has been misidentified as Lady Lavery, who did attend the trial with Sir Charles Beresford. Lavery wrote asking for details of the lady in the gallery, who was identified by Margaret Gavan Duffy as Eva Gore Booth (Margaret Gavan Duffy to John Lavery, Tate Archive, MS 7245). Quoted in 'Courting controversy: John Lavery and the Court of Criminal Appeal', in *High Treason: Roger Casement* (Dublin, 2016).

31 Lavery, *Life of a painter*, p. 208.

32 *Ibid.*, p. 63.

33 Lady Audrey Morris, unpublished biography of Lady Lavery.

34 Lavery, *Life of a painter*, p. 213.

35 Letter from John Lavery to Mrs Duncan, 14 July 1921 (Hugh Lane Gallery collection).

36 "Castle" referring to the seat of British Administration in Ireland at Dublin Castle.

37 Reproduced in Lavery, *Life of a painter*, p. 208.

38 This painting is in the Crawford Art Gallery, Cork. It is the opinion of the MacSwiney Brugha family that the likeness was taken from a photograph. There is no record of Sir John Lavery meeting Muriel MacSwiney.

39 Lavery, *Life of a painter*, p. 208.

40 *Ibid.*

41 Queen Mary purchased the study of the *Presentations of Debutantes to King George V and Queen Mary, the Ballroom of Buckingham Place*, 1932 (Royal Collection, RCIN 407135).

42 https://www.rct.uk/collection/themes/Trails/queen-marys-dolls-house.

43 Sir Shane Leslie's diary, 1914–1944 (National Library of Ireland, MS 22,863).

44 Sir Shane Leslie to Lady Audrey Morris, 15 June 1950 (Shane Leslie Collection, Georgetown University, Washington DC). Quoted in McCoole, 'Lady Lavery, her salon and its role in the emergence of the Irish Free State'.

45 Sir Shane Leslie's diary, 1914–1944 (National Library of Ireland, MS 22,863).

46 Sir Shane Leslie to Lady Lavery, 20 August 1921 (Shane Leslie Collection, Georgetown University, Washington DC).

47 Lady Lavery to Desmond FitzGerald (MS 49, 491/1/1461).

48 This is contained in the Michael Collins scrapbook (private collection) quoted in McCoole, 'Lady Lavery, her salon and its role in the emergence of the Irish Free State'. The other meetings noted in this scrapbook for 1922 all correspond to visits of Michael Collins to London.

49 He sat for his portrait for Lavery's Irish collection in 1925 (Hugh Lane Gallery).

50 Lady Audrey Morris, unpublished biography of Lady Lavery.
51 *Ibid.*
52 Art O'Brien to John Lavery (National Library of Ireland, MS 8425/7).
53 *Derry Journal*, 5 October 1921.
54 Michael Collins travelled over separately from the other members of the delegation, and lived separately with members of his squad.
55 Lady Lavery to Arthur Griffith (National Library of Ireland, MS 49,666/19).
56 John Lavery to Art O'Brien, 6 October 1921 (Robert Erskine Childers Collection, Trinity College Dublin, MS 7796/1/1).
57 The portraits of the British delegation were added to the Irish collection and donated to the Hugh Lane Gallery in 1935. These represent Winston Churchill (1915); David Lloyd George (1922); F.E. Smith, Earl of Birkenhead (1923); and Austen Chamberlain (n.d.).
58 Sir Philip Sassoon's office in Downing Street was given to the Irish delegation to use during the peace Conference.
59 Sir Shane Leslie's diary 1914–1944 (National Library of Ireland, MS 22,863).
60 Shane Leslie, *The long shadows* (London, 1966), pp 228–9.
61 Erskine Childers to John Lavery, 12 October 1921 (Robert Erskine Childers Collection, Trinity College Dublin, MS 7796/1/5).
62 Lady Lavery to Desmond FitzGerald (National Library of Ireland, MS 49, 491/1/1461).
63 This may be a reference to the fact that Desmond FitzGerald's wife Mabel had been secretary for George Bernard Shaw, who was a close friend of the Laverys.
64 Johanna (Hannie) Collins lived at 5 Netherwood, Shepherd's Bush. She and her brother had lived together during his time in London. See: www.generalcollins.com, article by TheNationalCollins22Society.
65 *The Sketch*, 2 November 1921.
66 The author had to go back to her confirmation record in Chicago in order to get the correct date to search for her birth certificate. On Lady Lavery's headstone there is an incorrect birth date of 1886.
67 Unidentified press cuttings, Lady Lavery scrapbooks, quoted in Sinéad McCoole, *Passion and politics. Sir John Lavery: the salon revisited* (Dublin, 2010), p. 50.
68 John Coville, *The Churchillians* (London, 1981), quoted in McCoole, *Hazel*, p. 58.
69 *Dundee Evening Telegraph*, 24 October 1921.
70 Exhibition catalogue, quoted in Lady Audrey Morris's unpublished biography of Lady Lavery.
71 See note 64, above.
72 Michael Collins to Kitty Kiernan, in León Ó Broin (ed.), *In great haste: the letters of Michael Collins and Kitty Kiernan* (Dublin, 1983), quoted in McCoole, *Hazel*, p. 75. The painting is known in a reproduction, signed by the artist and the sitter, which was sold in 1922. The portrait itself is missing; it was last known to be on an easel in the home of Kitty Kiernan. In correspondence with the author in April 1992, Felix Cronin, son of Kitty Kiernan, stated that the painting was not in the family's possession and that its whereabouts were unknown.
73 She had known Eddie Marsh from her earliest years in London; he had introduced her to Lady d'Abernon with a note to be nice to the little American woman (Lady Audrey Morris, unpublished biography of Lady Lavery).
74 Christopher Hassall, *Edward Marsh: patron of the arts* (London, 1959), quoted in McCoole, *Hazel*, p. 75.
75 Hazel Lavery to Clare Kennedy, 9 October 1922 (Kennedy Papers, University College Dublin Archives, p4/1434), quoted in McCoole, *Hazel*, p. 76.
76 John Lavery to J.H. Morgan, 14 December 1931 (Tate Archive, 7245.5), quoted in McCoole, *Passion and politics*, p. 63.
77 Lord Longford (Frank Pakenham), *Peace by ordeal* (London, 1972), p. 107, quoted in McCoole, *Hazel*, p. 75.
78 Trevor Wilson (ed.), *The political diaries of C.P. Scott 1911–1928* (London, 1970), pp 410–11.
79 Lady Audrey Morris, unpublished biography of Lady Lavery.
80 R. Erskine Childers to Mollie Childers, 6 December 1921 (R. Erskine Childers Papers, Trinity College Dublin MS 7865/1264), quoted in McCoole, *Hazel*, p. 81.
81 Robert Erskine Childers Diary, 6 December 1921 (Robert Erskine Childers Collection, Trinity College Dublin MS 7814/1102), quoted in McCoole, *Hazel*, p. 79.
82 'Standing by', *The Tatler*, 12 May 1948.
83 Oliver St John Gogarty, *As I was going down Sackville Street* (London, 1980).
84 *Larne Times*, 12 January 1935; *Belfast Telegraph*, 12 January 1935.
85 John Lavery to Art O'Brien, 6 October 1921 (Robert Erskine Childers Collection, Trinity College Dublin MS 7796/1/1). There is also a letter requesting access in the National Library of Ireland (MS 8,425/7).
86 *United Ireland*, 12 January 1935.
87 This includes providing Michael Collins with a pen-picture of the delegates (see Moya Llewelyn Davies to P.S. O'Hegarty, National Library of Ireland, MS 41,780).
88 Moya Llewelyn Davies to P.S. O'Hegarty, 8 June 1943 (National Library of Ireland, MS 41,780).
89 Josephine McNeill (née Ahearne) was the wife of the High Commissioner in London and Governor-General James McNeill. She was the first Irish female diplomat to represent Ireland in a ministerial capacity.
90 Moya Llewelyn Davies to Josephine McNeill, 13 September 1933 (University College Dublin Archive P234/117).
91 Lady Audrey Morris, unpublished biography of Lady Lavery.
92 Hannie Collins to Lady Audrey Morris, 26 August 1950 (copy in the author's collection).

Fig. 32: Sir John Lavery, *Shane Leslie* (1921).
Hugh Lane Gallery

John Lavery and national pictures

Fintan Cullen

A few days after the signing of the Anglo-Irish Treaty in December 1921, the writer and nationalist sympathiser Shane Leslie (Fig. 32) (1885–1971) contributed a short article entitled 'Sir John Lavery and the Irish Nation' to the *Irish Independent* in which he described a group of paintings by that artist. Leslie had doubtless recently seen them all in Lavery's London studio. Listing well over a dozen pictures, Leslie placed them in three categories, 'Laity', 'Clerics' and 'Scenes'. The first category included the Treaty portraits (see Cat. 3–12); the second comprised portraits of the Roman Catholic Primate of all Ireland, Cardinal Michael Logue (Fig. 33), and Archbishop Daniel Mannix of Melbourne; the final category listed such Lavery paintings as Roger Casement's appeal and the funeral of Terence MacSwiney (Figs 34 and 35). To Leslie, these paintings were 'the climax of [Lavery's] work', which, together with the portraits of Arthur Griffith and Michael Collins (Cat. 4 and 5), were 'national pictures'. Writing within a week of the signing of the Treaty, Leslie saw these images as both immediate and celebratory. His reference to the images as 'national pictures' would be repeated by other newspapers in the early years of the 1920s.[1]

Fig. 33: Sir John Lavery, *Cardinal Michael Logue* (1920).
National Museums NI, Ulster Museum Collection

Fig. 34: Sir John Lavery, *The Court of Criminal Appeal. London. 1916. (Roger Casement)* (1916).
Hugh Lane Gallery

Fig. 35: Sir John Lavery, *Southwark Cathedral, London, 1920 (Terence MacSwiney)* (1920). Hugh Lane Gallery

This essay questions Leslie's interpretation of Lavery's Irish paintings of the revolutionary period and his portrayal of them as 'national pictures', and argues that Lavery was more interested in events and the capturing of the historical moment than in offering insight or reflection. Lavery's relationship with the new Irish state in the 1920s will also be examined, along with a discussion of his output of the period and a comparison with one of his contemporaries, Seán Keating, in the context of that term 'national pictures'.

With his suite of Treaty portraits and his visualisation of significant occasions in the Irish revolution, John Lavery's 1935 bequest of 34 paintings to Dublin is a major component in any discussion of the representation of the foundation of the state. While born in Belfast, Lavery hardly ever lived in Ireland and Irish-themed images did not dominate his *oeuvre*, yet surprisingly, in the early 1920s, he was seen as potentially 'the official painter to the Free State'.[2] Artistically, financially and socially, Lavery did well out of Britain. In the 1920s and before he was a successful society painter, a war artist who was knighted in 1918 by King George V. He painted innumerable portraits of the British élite, from the *Royal Family* (1913; Fig. 24) to evocative interiors such as the *Van Dyck Room, Wilton* in Wiltshire (1920; Fig. 36).[3] How, then, should we see his relationship with Ireland's new-found independence after 1922?

Fig. 36: Sir John Lavery, *The Van Dyck Room, Wilton* (1920–1).
London, Royal Academy of Arts

While a frequent exhibitor at the Royal Hibernian Academy in Dublin and a Royal Hibernian Academician from 1906, it was in London that Lavery lived and made his mark.[4] He was a constant exhibitor at the annual exhibitions of the Royal Academy (RA) at Somerset House from the 1890s until his final exhibit in 1941, the year of his death.[5] In the 1920s, however, when so many of his now-renowned Irish paintings were produced, he only rarely exhibited an Irish painting in London, and none of the canvases listed by Leslie. Despite the production of all those Treaty portraits that were painted in London between 1921 and 1922, they were not shown at Britain's most prestigious exhibition space. In 1923 he did display at the RA portraits of William T. Cosgrave (Fig. 37) and James Craig (Fig. 38), the new leaders of the Irish Free State and of the Northern Ireland government respectively, but he did not show the now-well-known portraits of Griffith or Collins. In 1922 he did show a large canvas, *Viscount Morley moving the Address on the Irish Treaty in the House of Lords* (Fig. 19), which represents the rather subdued debate of the Anglo-Irish Treaty on 16 December 1921,[6] but, not surprisingly, he did not paint the comparable ratification of the Treaty in Dáil Éireann a month later, which was a far more 'emotive' occasion.[7] While throughout the 1920s he produced and displayed many society portraits at the RA, none of these were of Irish people—and that includes the many exhibited images of Hazel, Lady Lavery, who, despite her fantasies, was an American.

Fig. 37: Sir John Lavery, *William Cosgrave* (1923).
Hugh Lane Gallery

Fig. 38: Sir John Lavery, *James Craig, Rt. Hon. The Viscount Craigavon* (1923).
National Museums NI, Ulster Museum Collection

Lavery's Treaty portraits and other Irish-themed paintings were seen by Shane Leslie as 'a part of Irish history' put together 'as faithfully and fearlessly as the Four Masters once strove to do with pen in the seventeenth century'.[8] This analogy with the Four Masters—chroniclers of medieval Irish history—is unfortunate, given that scholarly opinion now sees the Annals of the Four Masters as being mostly based on pseudo-history. The Treaty, by contrast, did get signed and was enacted. While a proto-nationalist stance may lie behind the artist's wish to record the faces of the Irish negotiators of the Treaty and to paint scenes of enfolding events, such as the dead Collins (Fig. 21) or his funeral Mass in Dublin's Pro-Cathedral (Fig. 40), Lavery's often-expressed impartiality—a 'studied impartiality', as one art historian has put it[9]—asks us to pause before awarding him the accolade of painter of 'national' images. The Pro-Cathedral scene, for example, which was painted on 28 September 1922 from above the rear of the nave, is comparable in its dramatic use of the format of the high vantage point to earlier scenes, varying from a British royal procession passing London's Hyde Park corner only a couple of months previously, on 21 June 1922 (Fig. 39), to the aforementioned *Viscount Morley addressing the House of Lords of December 1921* (Fig. 19), or, two years earlier, the requiem Mass in Southwark Cathedral, London, for Terence MacSwiney (1920; Fig. 35).[10]

Fig. 39: Sir John Lavery, *A State Procession — the King, the Prince of Wales, the Duke of York and Prince George, Hyde Park Corner* (1922).
Priv. collection; Fine Arts Society. Photo © The Fine Art Society, London, UK / Bridgeman Images

Fig. 40: Sir John Lavery, *Pro-Cathedral Dublin 1922 (Michael Collins)* (1922). Hugh Lane Gallery

Be it a royal procession or an Irish nationalist event in Dublin or London, Lavery could paint it. His impartiality extended to painting both the living and the dead. While the poignancy of his celebrated 1922 painting of the dead Collins (Fig. 21) is heightened by our knowledge of Lavery's friendship with the commander-in-chief, such poignancy could also appear in one of his war paintings of a few years earlier, *The Cemetery, Étaples* (1919; Fig. 41), in which the rows of graves, pathetic wreaths dangling from wooden crosses and a passing train all conjure up an image of the waste of young lives.[11]

Fig. 41: Sir John Lavery, *The Cemetery, Étaples* (1919).
Imperial War Museum

Was Lavery's hesitation about showing too many Irish pictures at the Royal Academy a case of not wishing to provoke his British friends or to bite the hand that fed him? At least one Irish artist did exhibit a challenging Irish-themed picture at the RA in the 1920s. Seán Keating's (1889–1977) well-known *Night's Candles are Burnt Out* (Fig. 42) was exhibited in London in 1929 and offers us a complex account of post-independence Ireland.[12] With its cast of characters—the Catholic priest, the gunman, the capitalist, the drunkard, a dangling skeleton of the old Ireland juxtaposed with the model family of a mother, a father and two children looking towards the smooth concrete of the newly built hydroelectric station at Ardnacrusha on the River Shannon—Keating's painting poses questions. Keating's post-Treaty Ireland is not just about celebrating or recording factual history, a definite facet of Lavery's Irish paintings. Rather, *Night's Candles are Burnt Out* asks the rather blunt question: who owns this new future? While Lavery pictures are often smooth and even sharp, Keating has a raw, edgy quality to his finished work. Stylistically, both Keating and Lavery revered the academic tradition and both were staunch figurative painters who in their adherence to a visible painterly approach to the application of colour display a deep knowledge of past art, such as the work of the seventeenth-century Spanish artist Diego Velázquez (1599–1660). If we look back at Velázquez's great 1634–5 painting *The Surrender of Breda* (Fig. 43) and compare it with Lavery's *High Treason, The Court of Criminal Appeal: The Trial of Roger Casement* (Fig. 34) and Keating's *Night's Candles are Burnt Out* (Fig. 42), we see three big, detailed, visually impressive canvases, all carefully assembled and peopled. The narratives are clearly delineated, yet in the two twentieth-century paintings Lavery is precise, factual and straightforward, while Keating is equally easy to read but with a more complex meaning. Unlike the rather prosaic title of Lavery's painting, by using a line from Shakespeare's *Romeo and Juliet* Keating puts an onus on the viewer to work out a possible metaphorical meaning. Both Lavery and Keating were interested in representing tangible moments in time but their approaches to visual representation were very different. Years later, Keating was to recall that in the early 1920s he was keen to 'record the birth of a nation' and 'paint a full-time series of pictures of the people and events of those years', but he was thwarted by a lack of personal funds and what he called 'political bitterness'.[13] Lavery, by contrast, enjoyed a comfortable

Fig. 42: Seán Keating, *Night's Candles Are Burnt Out* (1928–9).
IVARO

Fig. 43: Diego Velázquez, *The Surrender of Breda* (1634–5).
Photographic Archive Museo Nacional del Prado

income and was little affected by political bias. Compared with his younger Irish contemporary, he did not have an assertive political stance. He was always on the fence, rarely critical and avoided complexity.

Prior to the Treaty portraits, Lavery had been producing Irish paintings. They include his two portraits of opposing prominent Irish political leaders, *Sir Edward Carson* and *John Redmond* (Figs 15 and 16), which the artist felt were 'a small contribution to unity for the sake of Ireland'.[14] In 1917 the paintings were presented, appropriately enough, in memory of Hugh Lane to what is now the Hugh Lane Gallery. Back in 1904, Lane had commissioned John Butler Yeats (1839–1922) to paint portraits of a host of Irish figures. In time, the series was taken over by William Orpen (1878–1931), and within a few more years all of these portraits by Yeats and Orpen were on display in Lane's newly established Municipal Gallery of Modern Art, which opened in January 1908.[15] In terms of Lavery's Irish subject-matter, the portraits of Carson and Redmond were soon followed by a Christian triptych, *The Madonna of the Lakes* (Fig. 44), which includes representations of his wife and their two children as, respectively, the Virgin flanked by St Patrick and St Brigid, all against a mountainous Irish landscape. The painting was presented to a Roman Catholic church in Belfast. As he wrote in his autobiography, in order 'to show the other side'

Fig. 44: Sir John Lavery, *The Madonna of the Lakes*, triptych.
Image courtesy of St Patrick's Parish, Donegall Street, Belfast

that he was not a bigot, Lavery then proceeded to present the Belfast Museum and Art Gallery with 'the original study for the Royal Portrait Group at the National Portrait Gallery', i.e. a group consisting of George V, Queen Mary, the Prince of Wales and his sister Princess Mary that had been painted a few years earlier (Cat. 13). Finally, Lavery was commissioned by his old acquaintance Sir Charles Darling, a Justice of the High Court, to paint *The Appeal of Roger Casement*. The large, finished version of the Casement picture (Fig. 34) never did find a home in Lavery's lifetime and was kept by the artist until his death. The smaller, less finished version became part of his Dublin bequest in 1935.[16]

Five years after Casement's appeal, Lavery would go on to paint his suite of portraits connected with the signing of the Treaty, as well as such canvases as *The Blessing of the Colours* (Fig. 45) and the dead Collins (Fig. 21). As with the Lane precedent of presenting portraits to Dublin, as a cultural phenomenon Lavery's 1935 bequest of pictures is not unique in the larger context of western art production. Visual celebrations of leading political players in national events had been painted and/or represented in Europe and North America for centuries. Most recently, in 1919 Orpen had produced a succession of portraits that contributed to his large *Signing of Peace in the Hall of Mirrors, Versailles* (London, Imperial War Museum), while back in the late eighteenth century John Trumbull had painted innumerable portraits of the signatories of the American Declaration of Independence.[17]

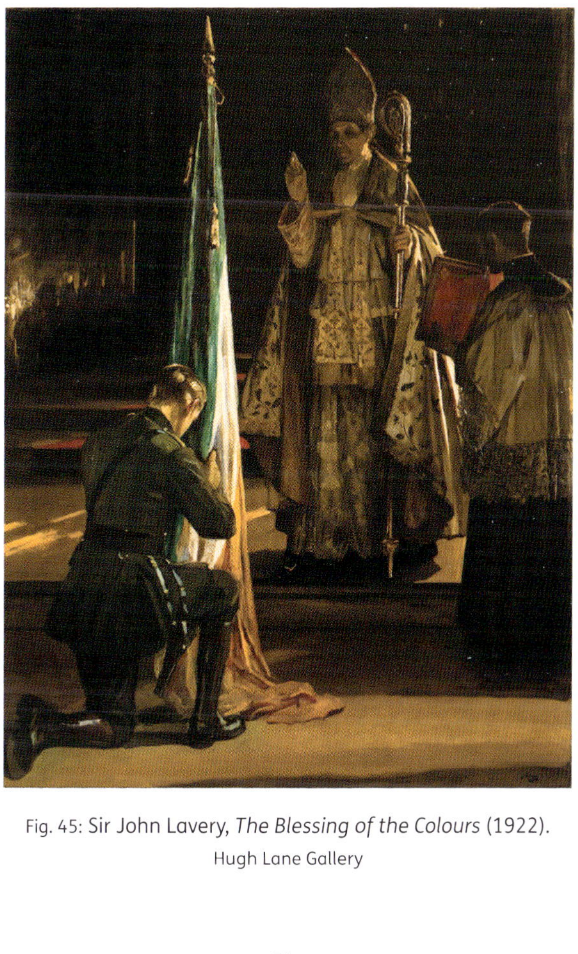

Fig. 45: Sir John Lavery, *The Blessing of the Colours* (1922). Hugh Lane Gallery

Many of Lavery's Irish paintings and the ones included in his Dublin bequest display a comparable rational approach to art production. They are painted in muted colours with a narrow tonal range; they represent authority and order, not discord or disharmony. As a young man in France in the 1880s, Lavery had perfected his craft by painting *plein air* scenes often effused with a dappled light (see *On the Loing, An Afternoon Chat*, also known as *Under the Cherry Tree*, 1884; Fig. 46). He maintained this French-inspired, naturalist style well into his mature years. Never one to dally with avant-garde artistic innovations, to which he must have had easy access in London in the first decades of the twentieth century, the artist was a traditionalist in a solid nineteenth-century fashion.

In the 1920s the Laverys developed close friendships with Collins, Cosgrave, Kevin O'Higgins and others associated with the first Free State government. In 1922 the artist was tipped as a possible governor-general of the Irish Free State, though that role eventually went to Tim Healy. A few years later he was commissioned by the Free State government to design the first Irish banknotes, which famously carried a portrait of Lady Lavery as a representation of Ireland.[18] For a number of years the Laverys regularly visited Ireland in August and attended the Royal

Fig. 46: Sir John Lavery, *Under the Cherry Tree* (1884).
National Museums NI, Ulster Museum Collection

Dublin Society Horse Show, with the artist even painting a picture entitled 'Hunter Class' (1926).[19] The couple were full of understanding in 1927 when Cosgrave's Cumann na nGaedheal government was cautious about going ahead with the first proposed Lavery bequest to the City of Dublin, given that it included 'portraits of living men who might reasonably object to their public and permanent display during their lifetime. A few of them would undoubtedly excite such feeling as might endanger their safety.'[20] A few years earlier, in 1923, such caution had not prevented the Laverys from attending the unveiling of a celebratory cenotaph (Fig. 47) erected on Leinster Lawn, overlooking Merrion Square at the rear of the new seat of an independent Irish parliament.[21] Designed by George Atkinson, Head of the Dublin Metropolitan School of Art, and built of cement, plaster and wood, the monument was a temporary structure, to be replaced over time. Plaster relief medallions painted to look like bronze by Arthur Power of the recently dead Griffith and Collins flanked a Celtic cross inscribed with the words *Cum Glóire Dé agus Onóra na hÉireann* ('For the glory of God and the honour of Ireland').[22] On 11 August 1923, the Laverys sat in the front row along with other dignitaries and members of the Free State government. Over the years the cenotaph has been criticised by historians and other commentators, and the underfunding of the monument has been much derided. By March 1926 the plaster-and-wood erection was 'peeling badly', and continuous repairs could not prevent the whole sorry heap from turning into an embarrassment. When a Fianna Fáil government was returned in 1932, plans were set afoot to build a new cenotaph, but nothing happened until after World War II. The original cenotaph, at the unveiling of which the Laverys were present in 1923, was removed in 1939.[23]

Back in 1921, Shane Leslie had suggested that Lavery's Irish paintings be 'presented to the Irish Nation as soon as the new Irish Government assign a habitation for the Arts on the banks of the Liffey'.[24] The paintings that make up the eventual Lavery bequest of summer 1935 largely date from the early 1920s. A time-lag of a decade and a half thus lies between their production and their eventual donation to Dublin. While Hazel Lavery died in January 1935 and although it is perfectly reasonable to acknowledge the gift by its official name, the 'Lady Lavery Memorial Bequest through Sir John Lavery, 1935', other issues beyond personal grief may have finally driven Lavery to give his collection of over 30 pictures to Dublin. When bequeathing his collection of Irish pictures, did Lavery wish to replace a peeling cenotaph to the achievement of Irish independence with his own undamaged bequest that included the portraits of Griffth and Collins? These paintings and the others were, and still are, in good condition, and when displayed to the public by the Dublin Gallery in February 1936 they were prominently exhibited in Charlemont House, the new home of Dublin's Municipal Gallery of Modern Art on Parnell Square in the centre of the city.[25] Since the peaceful transition to power by de Valera's Fianna Fáil party in 1932, any presumed pro-Free State taint that could be attached to Lavery—and, indeed, his bequest—was now fading. In addition, the

Fig. 47: George Atkinson, *Cenotaph to Michael Collins and Arthur Griffith on Leinster Lawn, Dublin,* cement, plaster, and wood (1923).
Image courtesy of the National Library of Ireland

bequest was pointedly displayed in the room left vacant for the contentious Lane gift of 'Continental' pictures held by London's National Gallery.[26] Lavery had the pleasure of hanging the pictures himself in a newly constructed top-lit gallery and, to prevent any damage to the pictures, each canvas was exhibited under protective glass.[27]

Kenneth McConkey, the leading commentator on Lavery, convincingly sums up the artist's career as that of a man who just wanted to paint, yet the question remains: *what* did he want to paint? While earning his living from society portraiture, Lavery also wanted to paint historical events, and Ireland, as his wife knew only too well, could offer him a particularly potent level of excitement. His painstaking attendance in 1916 at the Roger Casement appeal at the Central Criminal Court is an example of painting an 'event'. So, too, are the Treaty portraits and the painting of the dead Collins. While taking into account all the effort and time involved in executing such an admirable project as the Treaty portraits, these pictures do not make Lavery a 'national' artist, nor is the result a series of 'national portraits'. Rather, his Irish paintings are important recordings of events and a result of paying heed to Hazel Lavery's suggestion, made possibly around 1917, that her husband 'do something for [his] country'.[28] In the end Lavery did, but he also did plenty for the country in which he chose to live and work.

Acknowledgements

Given the constraints of the Covid-19 pandemic, I am most grateful to Logan Sisley, Róisín Kennedy and Billy Shortall for help with aspects of this essay. Special thanks also to Felicity Woolf.

Endnotes

1 *Irish Independent*, 12 December 1921, p. 4; *Freeman's Journal*, 14 August 1923, p. 4.
2 Sinéad McCoole, *Hazel: a life of Lady Lavery 1880–1935* (Dublin, 1996), p. 137.
3 For a full account of Lavery's career see Kenneth McConkey, *Sir John Lavery: a painter and his world* (Edinburgh, 2010).
4 For Lavery and the Royal Hibernian Academy in the 1920s see John Turpin, *History of the Royal Hibernian Academy of Arts* (2 vols, Dublin, 2018), II, chapter 3. Throughout the decade he exhibited many of the pictures that made up the eventual bequest to Dublin of 1935.
5 See 'The Royal Academy Summer Exhibition: A Chronicle, 1769–2018' (https://chronicle250.com/index/exhibitors/La-Lc).
6 *Sir John Lavery R.A. 1856–1941*, exhibition catalogue (Ulster Museum, Belfast/Fine Art Society, London, 1984), p. 86. John, Viscount Morley (1838–1923), was an elderly Liberal politician who had supported Home Rule under Gladstone and in Lavery's representation, the Viscount's last appearance in the Lords, he spoke in favour of the Treaty.
7 Diarmaid Ferriter, *The transformation of Ireland 1900–2000* (London, 2004), p. 243.
8 *Irish Independent*, 12 December 1921, p. 4.
9 Fionna Barber, *Art in Ireland since 1910* (London, 2013), p. 44.
10 See McConkey, *Sir John Lavery*, for details on all these pictures.
11 *Ibid.*, pp 141–2.
12 Éimear O'Connor, *Seán Keating: art, politics and building the Irish nation* (Dublin, 2013), pp 88–90 and *passim*. See also Sorcha O'Brien, *Powering the nation: images of the Shannon Scheme and electricity in Ireland* (Newbridge, 2017), pp 168–76.
13 Bureau of Military History WS0505, letter to Michael McDunphy, secretary to President Douglas Hyde and Director of the Bureau of Military History, 3 January 1951. My thanks to Logan Sisley for this reference. See www.militaryarchives.ie/collections/online-collections/bureau-of-military-history-1913-1921/reels/bmh/BMH.WS0505.pdf#page=10. For Keating's work of the early 1920s see O'Connor, *Seán Keating*, pp 127–35. and Róisín Kennedy, 'Art and uncertainty: painting in Ireland 1912–1932', in Brendan Rooney (ed.), *Creating history: stories of Ireland in art* (Dublin, 2016), pp 166–9.
14 John Lavery, *The life of a painter* (Boston, 1940), p. 207.
15 Fintan Cullen, *The Irish face: redefining the Irish portrait* (London, 2004), p. 65 and *passim*.
16 For these paintings see McConkey, *Sir John Lavery*, pp 130, 131–2. For the Casement painting see also Cullen, *The Irish face*, pp 205–9; Catherine Marshall, '"Of all the trials not to paint…": Sir John Lavery's painting *High Treason, The Court of Criminal Appeal: The Trial of Roger Casement*', in Lisa Godson and Joanna Bruck (eds), *Making 1916: material and visual culture of the Easter Rising* (Liverpool, 2015), pp 226–34; and Sinéad McCoole, 'Courting controversy: John Lavery and the Court of Criminal Appeal', in Jessica O'Donnell (ed.), *High Treason: Roger Casement* (Dublin, 2016), pp 17–23.
17 For Lavery's comments on Orpen's Versailles painting, see Lavery, *Life of a painter*, p. 148. For some of Orpen's Versailles portraits see Robert Upstone *et al.*, *William Orpen: politics, sex and death* (London, 2005), pp 43, 112, 113. For Trumbull see Helen A. Cooper, *John Trumbull: the hand and spirit of a painter* (New Haven, 1982), pp 76–81 and *passim*.
18 McCoole, *Hazel*, chapter 9.
19 James White and Kevin Bright, *Treasures of the Royal Dublin Society* (Dublin: Royal Dublin Society, 1998), p. 27, illustrated p. 41. See also McConkey, *Sir John Lavery*, pp 175, 240 n.120.
20 National Archives of Ireland/Department of the Taoiseach/s5503, Bodkin to Cosgrave, 28 July 1927. My thanks to Billy Shortall for this reference.
21 The attendance of the Laverys is captured on a short British Pathé news film; see https://ifiplayer.ie/cenotaph-to-michael-collins.
22 Síghle Bhreathnach-Lynch, *Expressions of nationhood in bronze and stone: Albert G. Power, RHA* (Newbridge, 2019), chapter 3.
23 Anne Dolan, *Commemorating the Irish Civil War: history and memory, 1923–2000* (Cambridge, 2003), chapter 1.
24 *Irish Independent*, 12 December 1921, p. 4.
25 *The Irish Times*, 15 February 1936, p. 19.
26 Róisín Kennedy, 'Art and uncertainty', pp 161, 171 n.24.
27 *The Irish Times*, 15 February 1936, p. 19. In 1927, when first considering a bequest of paintings, Lavery had stressed his preference for a 'top-lit gallery'; see NAI TAOIS/s5503, memo to Cosgrave dated 28 September 1927.
28 Lavery, *Life of a painter*, p. 207.

Recording the participants

Mick O'Dea

The portraits of the Irish treaty delegates were painted in the autumn and winter of 1921 in Lavery's studio at 5 Cromwell Place, South Kensington, not too far from 22 Hans Place, Knightsbridge, where the Irish delegates were staying.

The sittings were by appointment and must have offered the participants some respite from the arduous responsibility of determining the future relationship between Ireland and Great Britain. They were being recorded for posterity by one of the world's most renowned artists, who also happened to be Irish and who had set himself the task of being a witness and chronicler of this historic moment. Lavery's active engagement in Anglo-Irish affairs manifested itself after he attended the trial of Sir Roger Casement, where he was invited to record the appeal trial by the presiding judge, Sir Charles Darling. The final painting portrays a dignified Casement in the midst of the courtroom pageantry, his fate sealed in advance. Lavery left the painting in his will to the National Portrait Gallery and the Royal Courts of Justice, London, but after his death in 1940 neither institution was entirely comfortable hanging such a large 3m by 2m canvas which portrayed British justice in an ambiguous light and, if anything, appeared to be sympathetic to the accused. This very impressive painting is on permanent loan to the Honourable Society of the King's Inns on Henrietta Street, not very far from the Hugh Lane Gallery.

All the portraits of the delegates are painted on a dark ground, which facilitates the decision to eliminate any unnecessary background details, allowing the artist to get on with capturing the likeness in the shortest possible time. It is wet-on-wet or *alla prima* technique, a type of painting used by very assured painters of portraits. John Singer Sargent, Augustus John and William Orpen, to name only a few of Lavery's contemporaries, employed the technique.

The physicality of the paint application is just one of the pleasures in store when looking at these paintings. The paint is laid on with confidence and assurance, and the rich textures, standing proud at times, play with whatever available light is washing over the surface.

Lavery has positioned many of his sitters to receive the main illumination on the right-hand side of the face, with a lesser, reflected light on the left-hand side. There are exceptions, of course, such as in the treatment of Lloyd George, who faces the painter and therefore faces us directly, the light saturating his face. The paintings include torso, arms and sometimes hands, the latter often just about making it into the composition at the bottom of the canvas.

The Griffith portrait is a personal favourite of mine. Everything seems right about the composition and attitude. It has the characteristics of the other work, a sombre pallet for sombre suits in a blacked-out room. The lighting is dramatic and staged; the figure is almost *contre-jour*, with much of the face tonally in sympathy with the dark ground from which it emerges. The eyes are engaging; it is a very sympathetic portrait of the man.

Lord Birkenhead is painted resplendently in full military attire, displaying a chest of medals and honours. One half of his head and body is in the shade, and, as in the painting of his close friend Sir Winston Churchill, there is no reflected light on the left-hand side of his face. He hovers in the dark. Someone had to decide that he should be so dressed. I do not know the details surrounding that decision, but I feel that Lavery has not made the most of what must have been a very glittering display. In fact, it is remarkably subdued. Could it be that Lavery saw the man who prosecuted Sir Roger Casement over and above everything else?

Robert Barton was obviously too occupied to sit without going over his paperwork. He is the only one not 'just sitting' for his portrait; he has turned up on his own terms—no respite for this busy man. The painter has obliged him, but I am sure that he asked Barton to keep his head in the same position, assisted by the fact that the papers were one on top of the other rather than in book format, which would have necessitated the head moving slightly from left to right every time he moved on to a new page. It is an excellent study of concentration, painted at night with the assistance of warm electric lighting.

Charles Gavan Duffy and Eamonn Duggan, like Barton, have the appearance of having been painted in artificial light. They make a trio of paintings that look comfortable together.

Churchill, de Valera and Collins make another set. The Churchill painting is a study in contrast. It has the highest tonal contrast and one feels that the subject is totally at home in the situation.

I think that Duggan presented the biggest challenge to the painter, and in my estimation this work lacks the engagement that the artist had with the other portrayals.

De Valera in profile reveals little to us psychologically; it is a formal study of a statesman and we are fortunate that Lavery painted him. In the context of the Treaty negotiations, de Valera was not present; the 'ablest player' should not have been left in reserve, according to W.T. Cosgrave.[1]

The portrait of Collins is sensitive, with a touch of melancholy. The original has disappeared somehow, and the one we see was painted posthumously from a photograph. It has a poignancy absent in the other portraits.

Apart from the formal negotiations in the autumn of 1921, the delegates on both sides socialised informally as guests of Hazel and John Lavery at their Cromwell Place house and studio. Hazel in particular was a hostess who had influence and admirers in London, and she used her contacts in the establishment to bring people together.

We are fortunate to be able to engage with the portraits of these people in the Hugh Lane Gallery in Dublin. They will forever share the same stage together because of Lavery, offering us an alternative narrative to contemplate, immortalised in paint, part of our history and the history of art.

Endnotes

1 David McCullagh, 'Truce and Treaty: Why did de Valera not lead the delegation sent to London?', *The Irish Times*, 25 May 2021.

Treaties

David Godbold

For an unknown reason I have an entirely erroneous, perhaps filmic, version of the signing of the Anglo-Irish Treaty[1] playing in my head. It is approaching 2 a.m. on 6 December 1921 in a smoke-filled, men-filled room—it was the era of men after all, with the notable exception of some profoundly brave, ground-breaking women (Hazel Lavery, Maud Gonne) *behind* them. Otherwise it was the time of hats, misogyny and big coats. Arguably, 100 years later, it still is—just without the hats. Tumblers of whiskey and cigars to hand, the *men* protractedly struggle to agree mutually acceptable wording to bridge intractable differences. Finally, minute degrees of compromise push towards a sort of unhappy breakthrough: the plenipotentiary status of the Irish signatories *itself* casts the die for years of Irish political division, the horrors of civil war. Collins effectively signs not only the Treaty but also his own death warrant. And partition—never a solution—of the island of Ireland (Northern Ireland 'opts out') consigns it to a select group of the top 30 failed, politically imposed 'solutions' in world history, including India, Korea, Germany and Yugoslavia, to name but a few of the more recent examples. Kick the 'problem' down the road; put a plaster on a broken heart.

The reality was, of course, quite different from my construct. The opposing 'negotiators' hardly met face to face or all together, but from private rooms, with fear and suspicion, passed each other annotated typings that eventually closed a gap towards the point of compromise, a place actually envisaged by both Collins[2] and Lloyd George from the outset. Sort of. John and Hazel Lavery offered their London home 'as a neutral ground where both sides might meet' following the July 1921 truce. John took the opportunity to paint—and hence portraits of de Valera and Griffith evolved.[3]

What's a treaty, anyway? The *best* outcome can only be a reluctant agreement of a set of least-worst options. Maybe it's a bit like the rest of life, a wonder of little ironies making up a grudging dialectic, edging towards paradox. What would I know? I'm a Brit, after all—well, for the twenty-odd years of my life that I lived there. And despite studying, in the dark[4] of the late 1970s, Modern European History, (English) Literature—including a staked claim on the great Irish writers—and Art (at least that one stuck), we were not taught very much about our nearest neighbour, Ireland, other than the briefest mention of *it* as a 'problem'. Missing were all the details of effective colonial occupation; political, religious and cultural repression; economic and ecological exploitation; deforestation,[5] land-grabs and enclosure; absentee landlord*ism*, famine, and a prejudiced attitude of superiority to boot.

For the past number of years, a line from the great Irish playwright William Shakespeare (*right back at ya!*) has been knocking about my head—*'Love thyself last'*—and it has recently attached itself to the above filmic fantasy, as, while a perfect expression of *noblesse*, its selfless altruism feels antithetical, even contrary, to the pragmatic political realities that forge treaties. On further research, I find to my slight horror that, with heavy irony, it comes from Act III of *Henry VIII*,[6] as the king considers Cromwell's increasing political influence to facilitate self-seeking ends. The Cromwell in question here is, of course, Thomas rather than Ireland's nemesis Oliver, but Henry's personally motivated drive towards the English Reformation, the separation from the Church of Rome[7] and subsequent foundation of the Church of England with—surprise, surprise!—himself at its head hardly speaks to *last loving*. Its profound resonance was to hit Ireland like a tsunami, changing it forever. The birth of sectarianism and the pursuant persecution of Catholics arose ostensibly out of the desire for a divorce. One thing leading to another, in the wave of irony to paradox, the move against Irish Catholicism begets the violent disposition of the FitzGerald dynasty and the imposition of British control of the *Kingdom of Ireland* in 1541, with—once again, surprise!—Henry at its head. Flowing over nearly half a millennium of tribulation, a further paradox lies in the timing of the centennial of *The Treaty*, rubbing salt into the wound of the hard realities of Brexit, the Northern Ireland protocol, the respective impacts on the island of Ireland and a newly re-problematised relationship with the British government. Once again, it's difficult to see anyone involved in this latter-day self-partition loving themselves other than first. And after over 30 years of happy, unquestioned residence in Ireland, as exiled Brit/honor*ee* Irish, I now find myself in the process of negotiating to sign my own treaty, towards Irish nationalisation, if Ireland will have me. Why should they? What have *we* done? '… [*C*]*herish those hearts that hate thee: Corruption wins not more than honesty.*'[8]

Endnotes

1 Officially, the Articles of Agreement for a Treaty Between Great Britain and Ireland.

2 Nearly ten years earlier, Michael Collins had argued that the Treaty would give 'the freedom to achieve freedom'. David McCullagh,'Truce and Treaty: Why did de Valera not lead the delegation sent to London?', *The Irish Times*, 25 May 2021.

3 And as included in this historic exhibition and catalogue (Cat. 3 and 4).

4 In both attitude and power cuts.

5 Ah, the wonders of the British navy! Ever wonder where all that wood came from?

6 *Henry VIII*, or *All is True*, a late and little-performed history play, either written collaboratively with John Fletcher or finished by Fletcher after Shakespeare's death. The title *Henry VIII* appeared in the play's first published appearance in the 1623 *First Folio* … it sort of explains why I never read it—nor, I think, have many others.

7 In 1536.

8 *Henry VIII*, Act III.

Foreground, middleground, background

Niamh McCann

'… I turn into

A side street to try to throw off my shadow, and history

is changed'

Ciaran Carson, *Turn Again* (Belfast Confetti, The Gallery Press)

In the spring of 2021 I was invited by Logan Sisley, Acting Head of Collections at the Hugh Lane Gallery, to co-curate *Tableaux Vivants* as an exhibition in conversation with *Studio & State* at the National Museum of Ireland (NMI) Collins Barracks to commemorate the centenary of the 1921 Anglo-Irish Treaty. From the outset I was excited by the conversation, not least because I hold the view that all artworks and cultural artefacts sit within and arise from a landscape of context, gathering upon themselves layers of residual meaning that are part artistic intent, part aesthetic, part political influence and part layers of meaning accrued over time.

From a personal perspective, the counties north of the border and the Troubles have, both growing up and throughout my development as an artist, presented themselves as a difficult shimmering presence on the edge of my horizon. As a Dubliner, one feels very close to and yet distant from the reality and the consequences of a separating border. And still within my practice I have returned many times to the existence of this *edge* between North and South, situating works within the geographical and political landscape of Northern Ireland, a landscape that serves to question and foreground assumptions, context and meaning, identity and belonging; a landscape that is local and yet connected up to universal concerns.

Most recently, in a series of works acquired by the Hugh Lane Gallery—*Sculpture Picture Furniture Gesture #1–3*, a series first shown as part of *Furtive Tears* at the Hugh Lane Gallery in 2018/19—I explore physical tropes of power and intent within the context of the art artefact (and by extension our island histories) by looking at the subject of the body as it is portrayed in selected monuments. Specifically, I look to the iconic statues of James Larkin and Edward Carson, taking their famed hand gestures and folding these gestures, in turn, into objects that structurally mimic and point to older visual art histories ranging from Greek marbles to religious iconography.

What struck me most in approaching the selection of works for *Tableaux Vivants* was the opportunity to unpick how histories can be written, recoded and abstracted—inferred and held within the artefact—and how works held within the respective collections set subject-matter in relationship to the institutionalisation of the border on this island and to the setting up of national and cultural identifiers.

Over many discussions, Logan Sisley and I chose works from the Hugh Lane Gallery's collections that we believe act in conversation with the NMI exhibition and with the greater question of how artworks speak to histories, create histories and use visual languages to set up and reinforce power dynamics. Loosely, but carefully, we selected works for their contextual significance. We discussed how we might extend and deepen the questions provoked by the NMI exhibition, and offer a contrasting perspective, suggesting figurations as tropes, and revealing the interplay of gestural dynamics, as opposed the more directly intimate narrative suggested by traditional portraiture. We discussed how our selected works would function either in terms of a contemporary response to the Treaty signing and its consequences (as exemplified in the border works of Willie Doherty), or in terms of visual tropes that signal broad gestures of political conflict, such as the adoption of a mask or a gesture as a given shorthand of ideological intent (as signalled in Philip Guston's hooded figures).

Our aim was to select works that, seen side by side, offer an opportunity to reflect on the overlapping and sometimes contradictory experiences co-existent at the time of the 1921 Treaty. In Henry Scott Tuke's painting *To the Morning Sun*, the Christ-like pose of the light-dappled, joyous naked male figure stands in stark contrast to the solemn tones of Margaret Clarke's *St Patrick Climbs Croagh Patrick.* One work speaks forward in time to the politics to come, and the other to ancient landscapes (bringing to my mind the pre-Christian landscapes of Ireland).

In Lavery's *Blessing of the Colours* the problematic story of the Irish state is laid bare. A bishop blesses the upright flag proffered by the kneeling soldier, whom we might read as Michael Collins. In it I see the hope of the nascent state. I also see failures that we are still correcting, the handing over of power from one state to another and the complete absence of the female founders. This painting, in grand political style reminiscent of a Jacques-Louis David, sits alongside the gloriously raucous Isobel Gloag work *The Woman with the Puppets.* Gloag's reclining female nude, head thrown back in laughter, hints at the odalisques of Ingres and Renoir, and holds up her 'puppet' male figures in variations of conventional power suits (e.g. the lawyer, the banker, etc.). These puppets are mere swashes of paint, enough to be recognised as type but not as individuals. In contrast, the female figure is brought forth in luxuriant detail.

In bringing together *Tableaux Vivants*, we honoured the impulse and shared desire to create and unearth the often-difficult residues of historical narrative, meaning and power dynamics inherent in the art object. We sought to uncover a personal perspective on the political, suggesting gnarly, uncomfortable and sometimes perplexing or unresolved questions about how our own identities and histories are shaped and reflected by the objects we produce and choose to preserve.

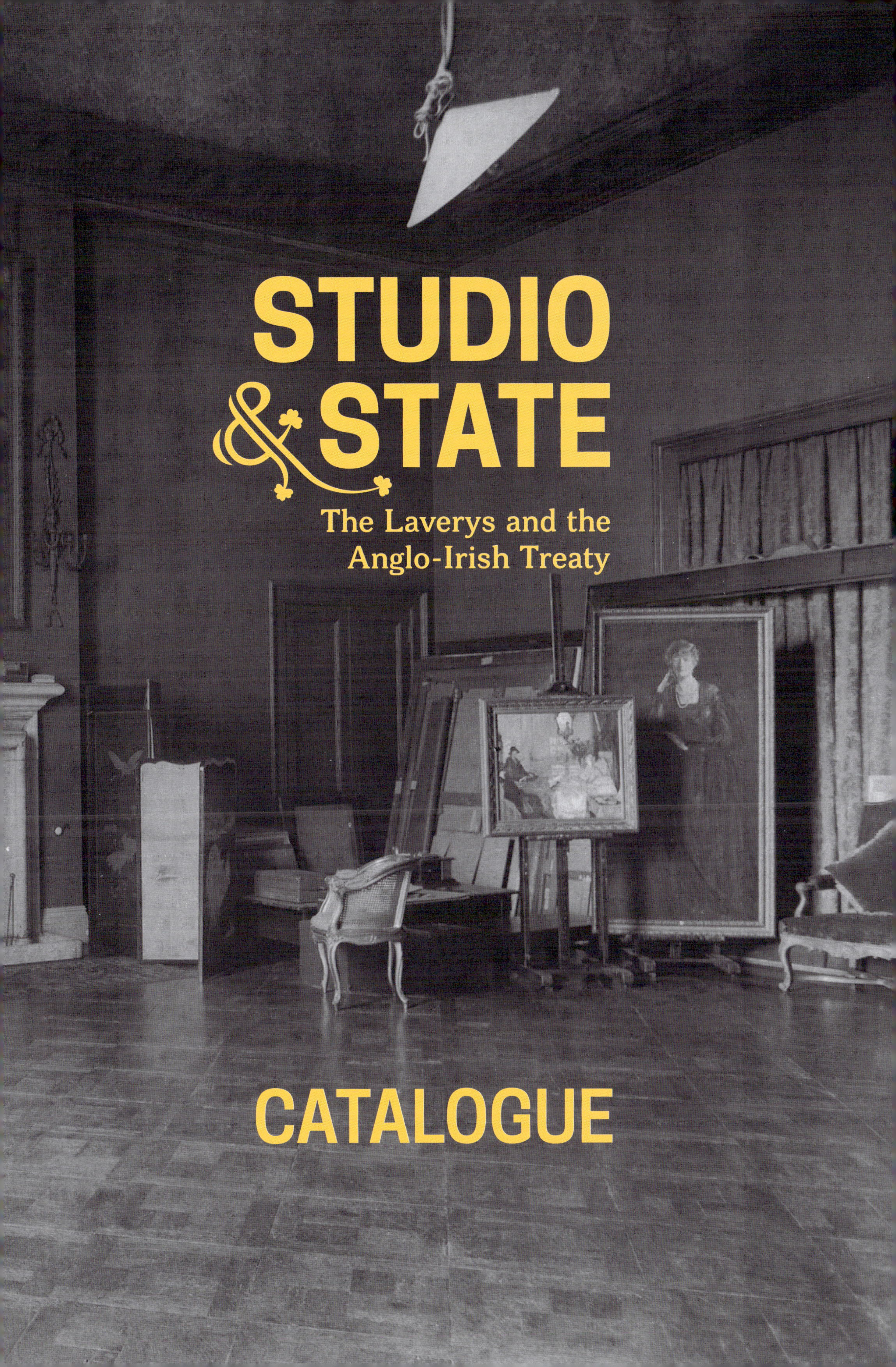

STUDIO & STATE

The Laverys and the Anglo-Irish Treaty

CATALOGUE

Cat 1:

Hazel, Lady Lavery

Sir John Lavery, 1921

Oil on canvas, 76.9 x 64.3 cm

Hugh Lane Gallery, Reg. 728. Lady Lavery Memorial Bequest through Sir John Lavery, 1935.

While Hazel Lavery did not pursue a career as an artist, she continued to sketch and paint after her marriage to John. This painting was included in the couple's joint exhibition at the Alpine Club, London, in 1921. In his introduction to the catalogue, Winston Churchill praised Hazel's 'natural facility', 'inborn sense of style', and 'native elegance'.

Cat 2:

Sir John Lavery

Mother and Child, 1909

Oil on canvas, 124.5 x 100.3 cm

Hugh Lane Gallery, Reg. 1222. Donated by Alice Gwynn, 1964.

Painted in the studio at 5 Cromwell Place shortly after Lavery and Hazel married, this is the earliest known portrait by the artist of his stepdaughter Alice and may be seen as Lavery documenting the arrival of his new family. John painted Hazel many times, which helped in the construction of her celebrated public image.

Cat 3:

Sir John Lavery

Éamon de Valera, 1921

Oil on canvas, 90 × 69.5 cm

Hugh Lane Gallery, Reg. 743. Lady Lavery Memorial Bequest through Sir John Lavery, 1935.

This portrait of Éamon de Valera (1882–1975), leader of Sinn Féin and President of the Dáil, was painted when he was in London for peace negotiations in July 1921. De Valera chose not to participate as one of the Irish plenipotentiaries in the peace conference from October to December that led to the signing of the Treaty. While Lavery wasn't entirely satisfied with this portrait and wished to make a second attempt, it was praised when first shown at the Paris Autumn Salon in November 1921.

Cat 4:

Sir John Lavery

Arthur Griffith, 1921

Oil on canvas, 76.9 x 63.9 cm

Hugh Lane Gallery, Reg. 730. Lady Lavery Memorial Bequest through Sir John Lavery, 1935.

Arthur Griffith (1871–1922) was a journalist and founder of the Sinn Féin party, but stepped aside as president in favour of de Valera in 1917. Griffith's portrait was begun in London during the peace negotiations in July 1921, which he attended as Minister for Foreign Affairs in the Irish Cabinet, having been released from prison weeks earlier. Following the ratification of the Treaty in January 1922, Griffith replaced de Valera as President of the Dáil, though this was short-lived, as he died in August of that year.

Cat 5:

Sir John Lavery

Michael Collins, c. 1935

Oil on canvas, 65 × 45 cm

Hugh Lane Gallery, Reg. 732. Lady Lavery Memorial Bequest through Sir John Lavery, 1935.

Lavery painted Michael Collins (1890–1922) during the Treaty negotiations but the original painting was given to Collins's fiancée Kitty Kiernan. Collins was killed in August 1922, during the Civil War that followed the Treaty ratification, and Lavery painted Collins lying in state and his funeral Mass at Dublin's Pro-Cathedral. The 1921 portraits of Collins and Griffith were published in an edition of signed lithographs to raise funds for Sinn Féin in 1922.

Cat 6:

Sir John Lavery

Gavan Duffy, 1921

Oil on canvas, 76.2 x 63.5 cm

Hugh Lane Gallery, Reg. 734. Lady Lavery Memorial Bequest through Sir John Lavery, 1935.

George Gavan Duffy (1882–1951) was born in England and had a successful legal career as a London solicitor prior to defending Roger Casement in his notorious 1916 treason trial. He then moved to Ireland, where he became involved in political life. He brought his legal expertise to the Treaty negotiations, which he signed because he saw 'no rational alternative'.

Cat 7:

Sir John Lavery

Éamonn J. Duggan, 1921

Oil on canvas, 76.8 x 64.6 cm

Hugh Lane Gallery, Reg. 731. Lady Lavery Memorial Bequest through Sir John Lavery, 1935.

Éamonn (Edmund) John Duggan (1878–1936) was a solicitor turned politician whose role in the Irish delegation was to liaise with British officials. Duggan and Barton made arrangements for the signing of the Truce earlier in 1921 and Duggan's appeal to the reluctant Barton helped persuade the latter to sign the Treaty.

Cat 8:

Sir John Lavery

Robert Barton, 1921

Oil on canvas, 76.2 x 63.6 cm

Hugh Lane Gallery, Reg. 733. Lady Lavery Memorial Bequest through Sir John Lavery, 1935.

Robert Barton (1881–1975) was Minister for Economic Affairs in the Dáil and was included in the Irish delegation for his economic expertise. While he signed the Treaty, he later campaigned against it. Barton's cousin, Erskine Childers, was secretary to the Irish delegation and also opposed the Treaty.

Cat 9:

Sir John Lavery

David Lloyd George, 1922

Oil on canvas, 76.2 x 63.6 cm

Hugh Lane Gallery, Reg. 735. Lady Lavery Memorial Bequest through Sir John Lavery, 1935.

Liberal Party leader David Lloyd George (1863–1945) became Prime Minister of the coalition government in 1916 and led the British delegation negotiating the Anglo Irish Treaty. Lavery was knighted under Lloyd George's government in 1918 for his services as a war artist and in his autobiography he praised the Prime Minister as taking pride of place among the politicians he had befriended. He painted Lloyd George again in 1935.

Cat 10:

Sir John Lavery

Sir Winston Churchill, 1915

Oil on canvas, 76.8 x 63.9 cm

Hugh Lane Gallery, Reg. 737. Lady Lavery Memorial Bequest through Sir John Lavery, 1935.

Sir Winston Spencer Churchill (1874–1965) was Secretary of State for the Colonies at the time of the Treaty negotiations. The Churchills were close friends of the Laverys. Winston was a keen amateur artist and received instruction in painting from John and Hazel. Churchill did not sit for Lavery during the Treaty negotiations, so John included this earlier portrait in his group of Treaty signatories.

Cat 11:

Sir John Lavery

Sir Austen Chamberlain, 1921

Oil on board, 75.9 × 63.3 cm

Hugh Lane Gallery, Reg. 738. Lady Lavery Memorial Bequest through Sir John Lavery, 1935.

At the time of the Treaty negotiations, Austen Chamberlain (1863–1937) was leader of the Conservative Party, which was in coalition with the Liberal Party led by Lloyd George. Intriguingly, his portrait is unfinished, giving an insight into Lavery's painting process. The reason for this is unclear, as the Laverys and the Chamberlains mixed in the same social circles.

Cat 12:

Sir John Lavery

The Earl of Birkenhead, 1923

Oil on canvas, 76.2 × 63.6 cm

Hugh Lane Gallery, Reg. 736. Lady Lavery Memorial Bequest through Sir John Lavery, 1935.

Lavery's portrait of Frederick Edwin Smith, first Earl of Birkenhead (1872–1930), then Lord Chancellor of Great Britain, stands out among the Treaty paintings as he appears in court dress. He is shown wearing the levee dress coat, with his army medals pinned to his chest. Birkenhead was unpopular in Ireland, in part for his role in prosecuting Roger Casement for treason in 1916, which led to unease when Lavery first proposed giving his Treaty portraits to Dublin in the 1920s.

Cat 13:

Sir John Lavery

Second Study for the King, the Queen, the Prince of Wales, the Princess Mary, Buckingham Palace, 1913

Oil on canvas, 76.1 x 63.4 cm

Ulster Museum, BELUM.U615. Gift of the artist, 1919.

This is a study for the monumental painting *The Royal Family at Buckingham Palace*, 1913 (National Portrait Gallery, London), which was commissioned by publisher W.H. Spottiswoode. It shows King George V and Queen Mary with two of their children, Prince Edward, Duke of Windsor (later King Edward VIII), and Princess Mary (later Countess of Harewood).

Cat 14:

Sir John Lavery

The Ratification of the Irish Treaty in the English House of Lords, 1921

Oil on board, 36 x 26 cm

National Gallery of Ireland, NGI.1736. Purchased, 1963.

The Treaty was ratified by the British Houses of Parliament in December 1921 and by the Dáil in January 2022. Lavery was the first artist to get permission to paint in the British House of Lords, where he spent three days making studies of the general scene and of individual figures. Lavery's completed painting of the scene, *Viscount Morley Addressing the House of Lords*, 1921–1922, was acquired by Glasgow Museums shortly after completion.

Cat 15:

Sir John Lavery

Lady Lavery in an Evening Cloak, c. 1918 or c. 1935

Oil on canvas, 46 x 36 cm

National Gallery of Ireland, NGI.1251. Presented, 1953.

This is a smaller version of Lavery's large-scale painting *Hazel in Rose and Gold*, 1918 (Walker Art Gallery, Liverpool). It is either a preparatory sketch for the 1918 painting or a memento of Hazel painted after her death. John Lavery gave the work to Eddie Marsh, Churchill's secretary at the time of the Treaty, who had been a friend of Hazel since 1909.

Cat 16:

Unknown Artist

Life Mask of Sir John Lavery, RA, 1930

Bronze, 44 × 18 × 21 cm

Hugh Lane Gallery, Reg. 698. Donated by Sir John Lavery, 1933.

John Lavery gave the gallery this life mask two years before he donated the portrait of the 'artist donor' by Hazel and 33 of his own paintings in memory of Lady Lavery in 1935. A life mask is made from the mould of the face of a living person.

No 1020 KENSINGTON.

5, CROMWELL PLACE.
S.W.7.

LIST OF PICTURES PRESENTED AS A FREE GIFT TO THE CITY OF DUBLIN
IN MEMORY OF LADY LAVERY BY HER HUSBAND.

****

1. John Lavery by Hazel Lavery.
2. Timothy O'Healy.
3. Arthur Griffith.
4. Michael Collins.
5. E.S.O.Duggan.
6. Robert Barton.
7. Gavan Duffy.
8. David Lloyd George.
9. The Earl of Birkenhead.
10. Winston Churchill.
11. Sir Austen Chamberlain.
12. Major Compton Smith (Posthumous).
13. William Cosgrave.
14. Archbishop Mannix.
15. Kevin O'Higgins.
16. Eamon de Valera.
17. Michael Collins (Love of Ireland)
18. Hugh Nihill Kennedy.
19. Sir Horace Plunket.
20. The Earl of Dunraven.
21. Viscount Northcliffe.
22. George Bernard Shaw.
23. Shane Leslie.
24. Pro Cathedral.........Dublin 1922.
25. Southwark Cathedral....London 1920.
26. Court of Criminal Appeal.....London 1916.
27. The First Irish Air-Woman.
28. Air Alfred Cope.
29. The Blessing of the Colours. — already sold, 1933
30. Count John MacCormack and his Family.
31. Hazel Lavery by John Lavery.
32. St. Patrick's Purgatory.
33. The Unfinished Harmony. 1934.
34. It is Finished. 4th. January 1935.

****

Cat 17:

Typescript list of pictures given by Sir John Lavery to the Municipal Gallery of Modern Art (now Hugh Lane Gallery) in memory of Hazel, Lady Lavery, 1935.

Hugh Lane Gallery Archive.

Cat 18:

David Wilson

Sir John Lavery, c. 1912

Ink on paper, 35.1 x 26 cm

Hugh Lane Gallery, Reg. 980. Donated by Joseph Holloway, 1943.

David Wilson grew up in Belfast but established himself as a cartoonist in London for the *Daily Chronicle*, *Tatler*, *Punch* and the *London Opinion*, among other publications. While the publication details of this particular caricature have not been identified, the Belfast satirical magazine *Nomad's Weekly* on 28 June 1913 published an article asking why John Lavery was not honoured in his home city when "all London is flocking to see" his portrait of the Royal Family, the study for which (cat. 13) the artist later gave to the Ulster Museum.

Cat 19:
Photograph of the scene outside the Mansion House, Dublin, during the Anglo-Irish Truce negotiations on 8 July 1921. Two American flags are visible amongst the crowd.
NMI HE:EWL.104

Cat 20:
General Macready arriving for truce negotiations at the Mansion House, Dublin, July 1921.
NMI HE:EW.102

TRUCE
JULY 1921

Cat 21:
Arthur Griffith and Éamon de Valera leave the Mansion House, Dublin, following truce negotiations in July 1921.

NMI HE:EWP.147

This image is part of the Joseph Cashman collection of photographs, which was purchased by the National Museum of Ireland in 1942.

Cat 22:

Typewriter

NMI HE:EWP.147

This Underwood typewriter was used to type Irish versions of letters from the Irish to the English government, leading up to the truce in July 1921. These Irish-language letters were typed by Séamus MacConglinne, who later became Secretary of Conradh na Gaeilge (the Gaelic League). Conradh na Gaeilge had purchased the typewriter about 1905 and it was probably the first ever made with Irish lettering.

SPECIAL ISSUE.
VOLUME 5. NUMBER 28. IRISH BULLETIN. SATURDAY. 9TH JULY.1921.

The following general order has been issued by the General Headquarters of the Irish Republican Army:-

OGLAIGH NA H-EIREANN.

G.H.Q.
DUBLIN.

GENERAL ORDER.

TO:
Officers Commanding
All Units.

In view of the conversations now being entered into by our Government with the Government of Great Britain, and in pursuance of mutual understandings to suspend hostilities during these conversations, active operations by our troops will be suspended as from Noon Monday, July Eleventh.

RISTEARD UA MAOLCHATHA.

CHIEF OF STAFF.

9/7/1921.

President de Valera has issued the following Proclamation:-

PROCLAMATION.

Fellow-citizens,

During the period of the truce each individual soldier and citizen must regard himself as a custodian of the nation's honour.

Your discipline must prove in the most convincing manner that this is the struggle of an organised nation.

In the negotiations now initiated your representatives will do their utmost to secure a just and peaceful termination of this struggle, but history, particularly our own history, and the character of the issue to be decided are a warning against undue confidence.

An unbending determination to endure all that may still be necessary, and fortitude such as you have shown in all your recent sufferings -- these alone will lead you to the peace you desire.

Should force be resumed against our nation, you must be ready on your part once more to resist. Thus alone will you secure the final abandonment of force, and the acceptance of justice and reason as the arbiter.

EAMON DE VALERA.

July 9th 1921.

Cat 23:

Copy of the *Irish Bulletin*, no.28, vol.5, 9 July 1921

NMI HE:EW.705

This issue of the *Irish Bulletin* contains the order, issued by the Irish Republican Army's headquarters, to 'suspend hostilities' from 11 July 1921 and a copy of the Proclamation by President Éamon de Valera. He assures 'fellow-citizens' that 'your representatives will do their utmost to secure a just and peaceful termination of this struggle (...)'. Five issues of the *Irish Bulletin* were produced each week during the War of Independence by the Irish Department of Propaganda. From February 1921, the *Bulletin* was edited by Erskine Childers, who was then Director of Propaganda.

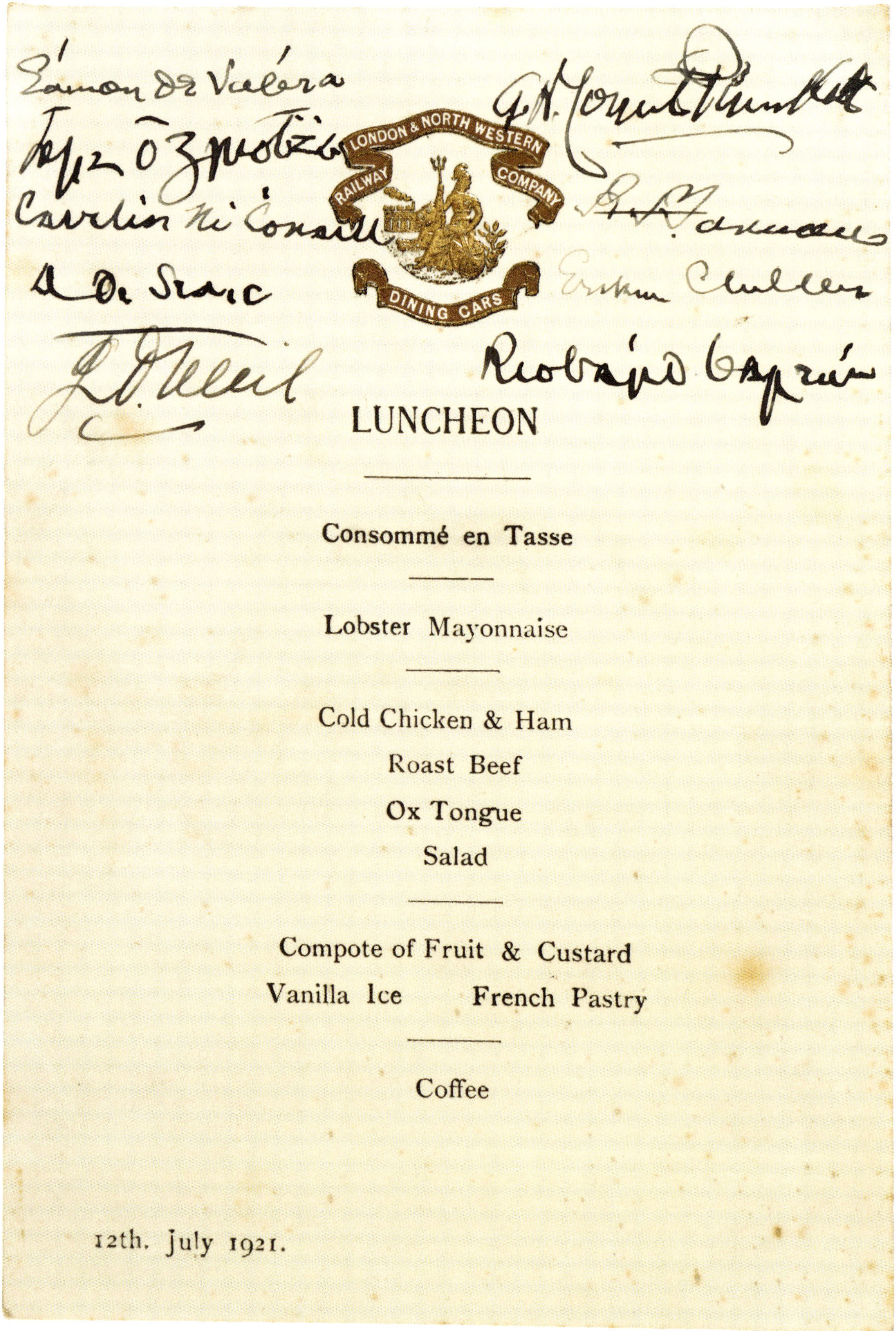

LUNCHEON

Consommé en Tasse

Lobster Mayonnaise

Cold Chicken & Ham
Roast Beef
Ox Tongue
Salad

Compote of Fruit & Custard
Vanilla Ice French Pastry

Coffee

12th. July 1921.

Cat 24:

< Lunch Menu Card, 12 July 1921

NMI HE:1995.33 (temp.)

Following the truce, an Irish delegation set off on 12 July 1921 aboard the Royal Mail steamer and train to London in order to lead talks with the British government to negotiate an Anglo-Irish Treaty.
Aboard the train, the delegates kept this menu card with the London and North Western Railway Company logo. It lists the options for that day's lunch, including lobster mayonnaise and ox tongue. The menu also bears the signatures of the delegates, including Éamon de Valera, Arthur Griffith, Kathleen O'Connell, Austin Stack, Robert Barton (all signed in Irish), Laurence O'Neill, Count George Plunkett and Erskine Childers.

Cat 25:
Robert Barton, Éamon de Valera, Count George Noble Plunkett, Arthur Griffith and Erskine Childers *(from left to right)* on board ship on their way to London, 12 July 1921.

NMI HE:EW.2571

Cat 26:
This photograph was taken at the Grosvenor Hotel, London, showing the first Irish Peace Delegation shortly after arrival in July 1921.
Sitting: Éamon de Valera and Arthur Griffith.
Standing, left to right: Count George Noble Plunkett, Erskine Childers, Laurence O'Neill (Lord Mayor of Dublin), Miss Lily O'Brennan, Dr Robert Farnan and his wife Lora Farnan, Robert Barton and Miss Kathleen O'Connor (de Valera's secretary).

NMI HE:EW.111.1

La foule massée près de la barrière dressée en avant du n° 10 de Downing street, pour voir l'arrivée de M. de Valera qui va conférer avec M. Lloyd George.

Cat 27:
This photograph has been reproduced from a newspaper clipping. It depicts crowds gathering at 10 Downing Street, London, ahead of the negotiations between Irish and British delegates in July 1921.
NMI HE:1997.107.4 (temp.)

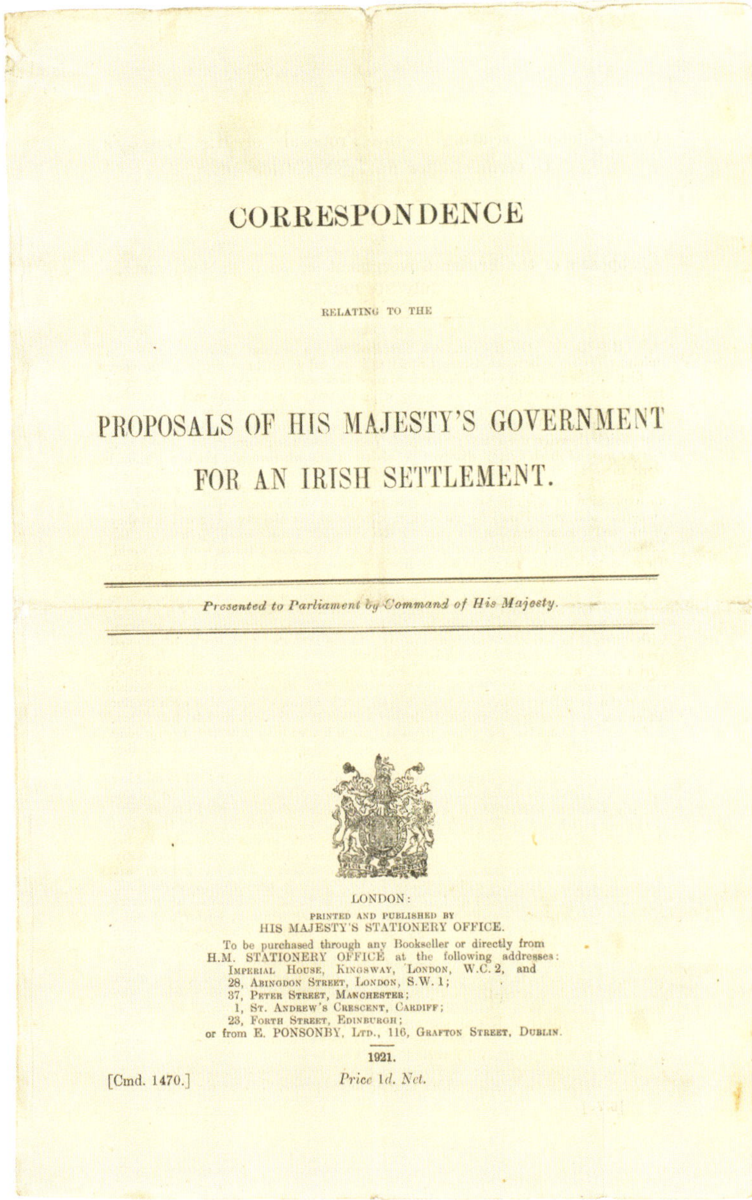

Cat 28:

British Stationery Office Publication: Correspondence relating to the *Proposals of H.M. Government for an Irish Settlement*, 1921

NMI HE:EW.24.3 (purch.)

During the talks in July, de Valera and Lloyd George did not reach an agreement but they committed to keeping the lines of communication open. This publication includes a reprinted letter by Lloyd George to de Valera, dated 20 July 1921, proposing the terms of the British government 'for an Irish settlement'.

In his response, dated 10 August, de Valera rejects the proposed Irish dominion status within the British Empire, seeking self-determination outside of the British Empire and 'amicable but absolute separation'. Lloyd George responds on 13 August: 'No such right can ever be acknowledged by us'. He concludes: 'Our proposals present to the Irish people an opportunity such as has never dawned in their history before (...)'.

TREATY NEGOTIATIONS OCTOBER - DECEMBER 1921

Cat 29:
Members of the Treaty delegation photographed at Holyhead on their way to London, October 1921.
Front row, left to right: Arthur Griffith, May Duggan, George Gavan Duffy. Second row, centre: Éamonn Duggan and Robert Barton *(right)*. *Top right-hand corner:* Kathleen McKenna, Ellie Lyons and (probably) Lily O'Brennan.
Cashman Collection.
NMI HE:EWP.146

Cat 30:

Gaming sheet and rack. Roulette wheel

NMI HE:EW.4202a-b

This gaming set was donated to the National Museum of Ireland in 1972. The donor's father had bought it for the entertainment of the Anglo-Irish Treaty delegation and staff in London in 1921. It comprises a canvas number sheet, croupier's rake and spinning roulette in a wooden frame.

Cat 31:

Rubber stamp

IE-MA-AL-CC-02-47 (Ceannt Collection), Brother Allen Collection, Military Archives

Stamp used during the Treaty negotiations in the autumn of 1921 to mark documents as 'SECRET'.

Photo © Military Archives

Cat 32:

Autograph book, Irish Delegation of Plenipotentiaries, 16 October 1921

NMI HE:1997.91 (temp.)

In the first half of the twentieth century, autograph books such as this were a common means to collect the signatures of friends and family or those present at important social or political events. They also survive from World War One internment camps and the Irish Civil War (1922–1923). This page bears the Irish autographs of the Irish Treaty delegates: Art Ó Gríobhtha, Riobárd Bartún, Seoirse Gabhán Ó Dubhthaigh, E. S. Ó Dúgáin and Mícheál Ó Coileáin.

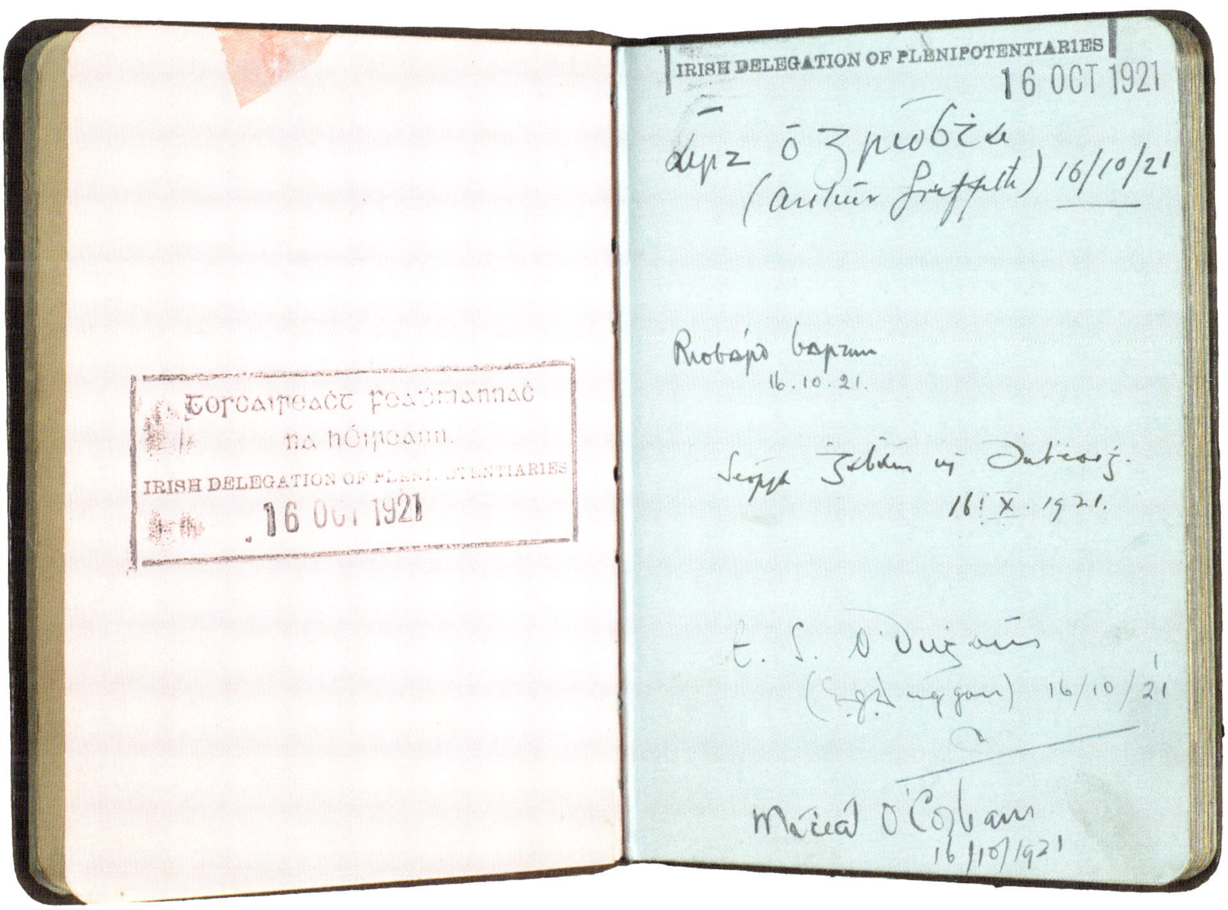

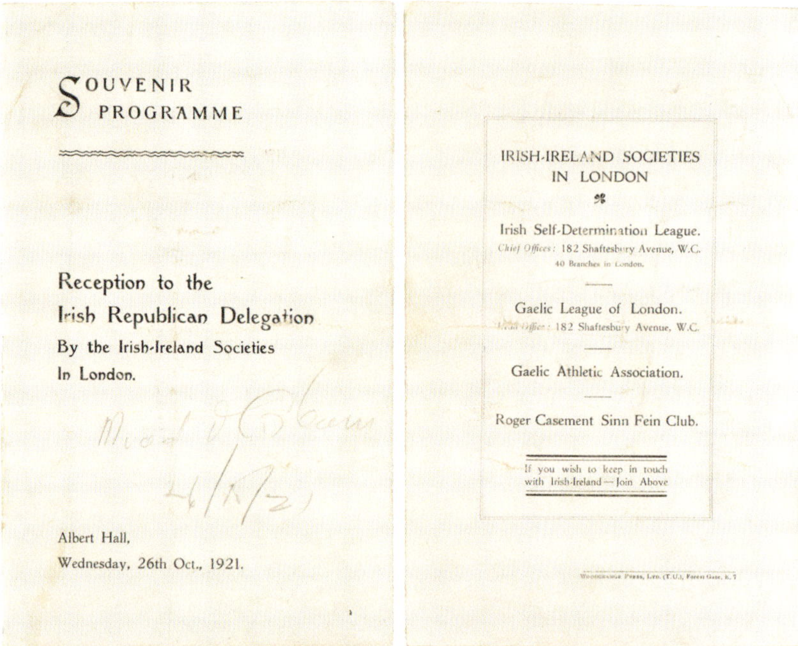

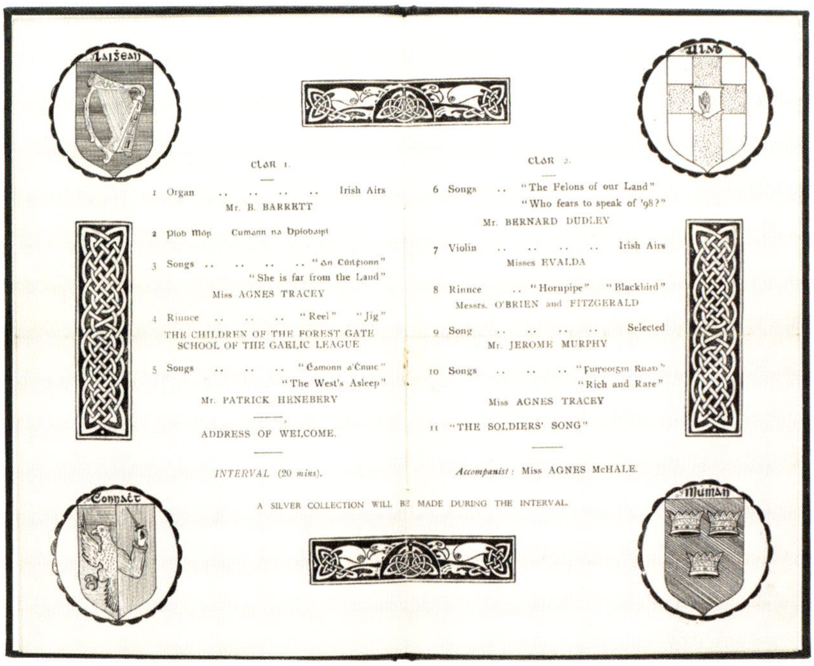

Cat 33:

Souvenir programme

HE:EW.Temp.95 and NMI HE:EW.702

This is a souvenir of the 'Reception to the Irish [Treaty] Delegation', which was organised by the Irish-Ireland Societies in London and took place at the Royal Albert Hall on Wednesday, 26 October 1921. The copy of the programme pictured at the top of this page was autographed by Michael Collins on the same day. The programme features Irish dance, music and songs, such as *Who fears to speak of '98* and *The soldier's song*. The latter was adopted as Ireland's National Anthem in 1926.

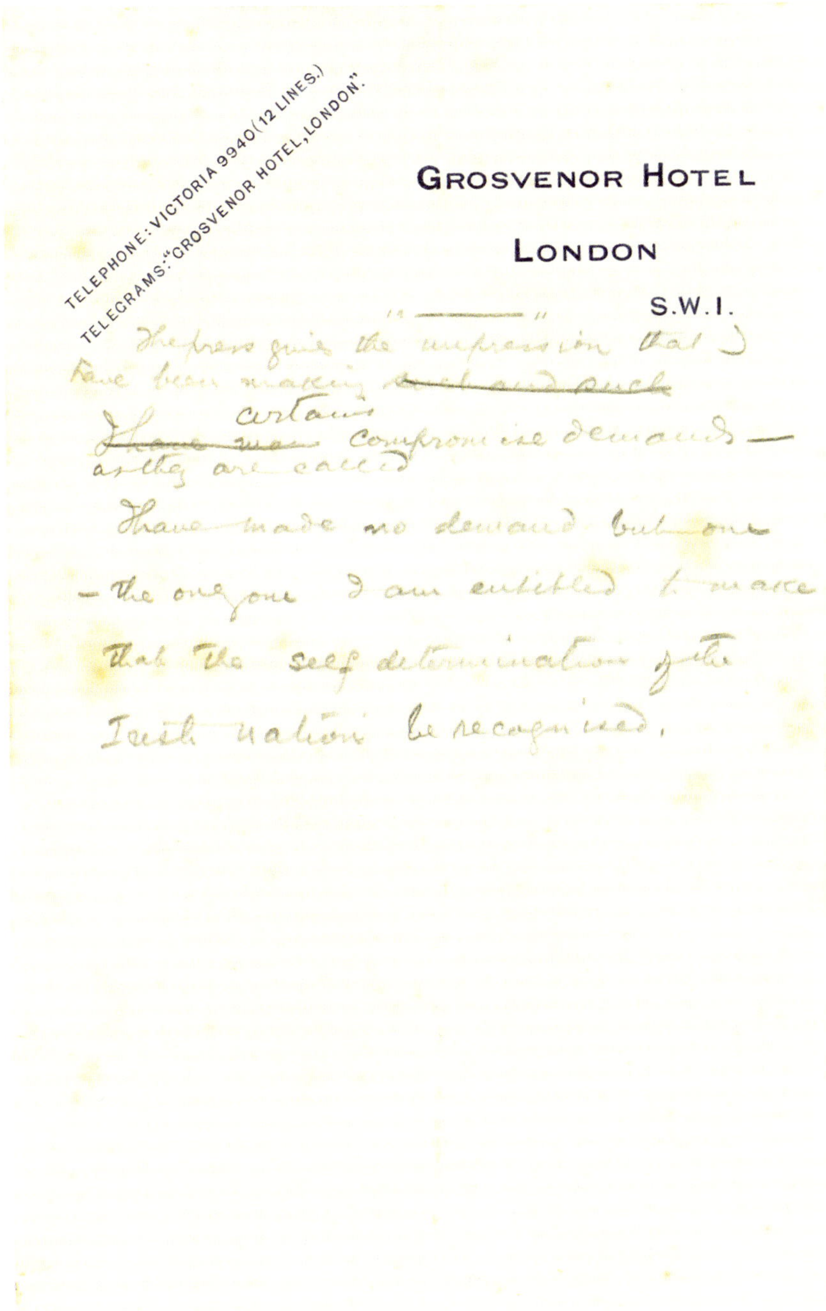

TELEPHONE: VICTORIA 9940 (12 LINES.)
TELEGRAMS: "GROSVENOR HOTEL, LONDON".

GROSVENOR HOTEL

LONDON

S.W.I.

The press give the impression that I have been making certain compromise demands — as they are called

I have made no demand but one — the one one I am entitled to make that the self determination of the Irish nation be recognised.

Cat 34:

Handwritten note, 1921

NMI HE:EW.Temp.230

The Irish delegation set up the headquarters at the Grosvenor Hotel, 22 Hans Place, in London during the Treaty negotiations, where this note was written in pencil on headed hotel paper, probably by Michael Collins. It reads: 'The press gives the impression that I have been making certain compromise demands — as they are called. I have made no demand but one — the only one I am entitled to make [—] that the self-determination of the Irish nation be recognised.'

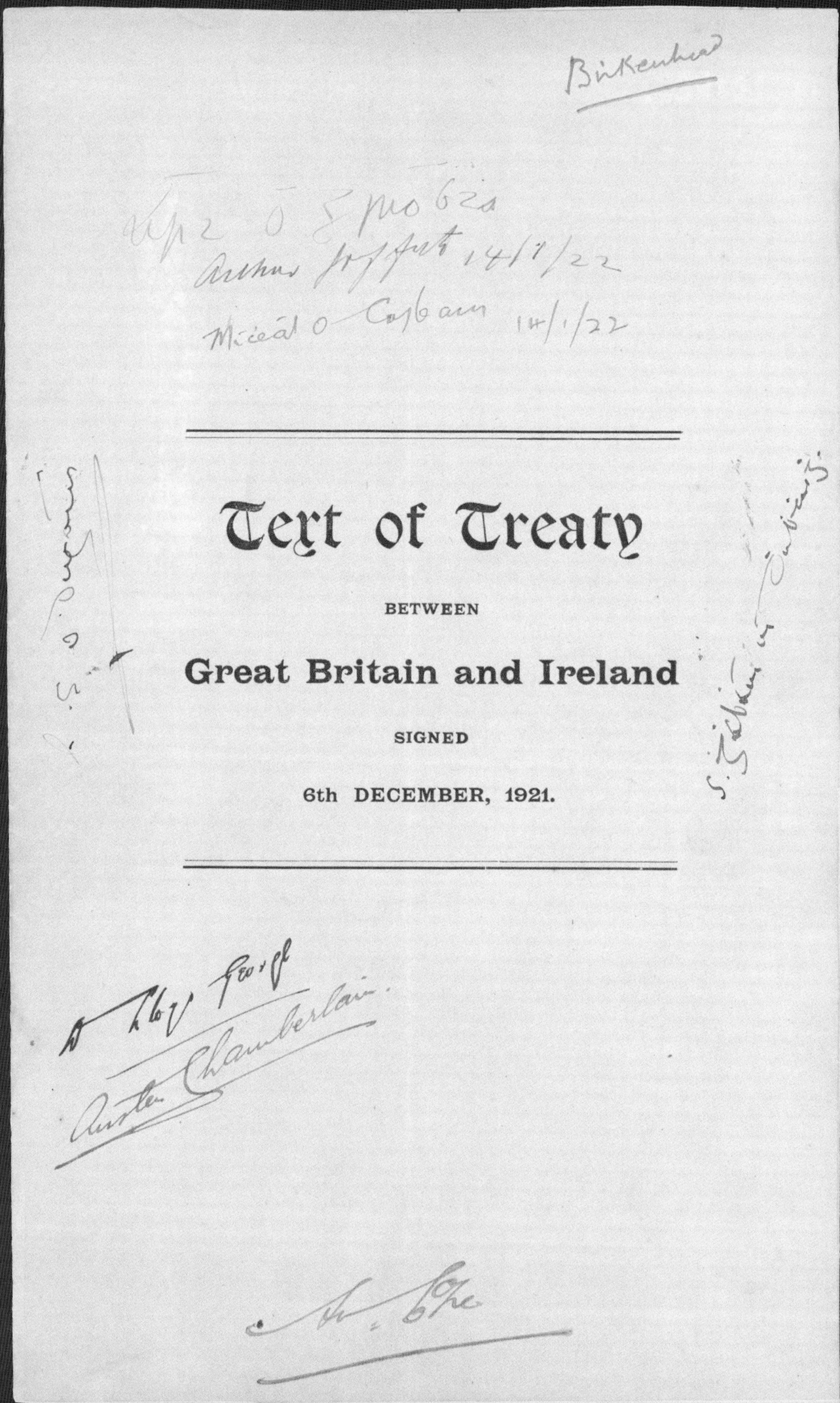

Text of Treaty

BETWEEN

Great Britain and Ireland

SIGNED

6th DECEMBER, 1921.

Cat 35:

< Autographed copy of the 1921 Anglo-Irish Treaty

NMI HE:EW.4037

The original copy of the Anglo-Irish Treaty was signed at 10 Downing Street at 2.20 a.m. on 6 December 1921 by seven British delegates and five Irish delegates.
This printed copy of the Treaty contains the full text of the original document, including the eighteen 'Articles of Agreement', which gave Ireland — 'to be styled and known as the Irish Free State' — dominion status within the British Empire.
It bears the autographs of eight of its signatories: Art Ó Gríobhtha, Arthur Griffith, Mícheál Ó Coileáin [both dated 14 January 1922], E.S. Ó Dugáin, S. Gabháin Ua Dhubhthaigh, Birkenhead, D. Lloyd George, Austen Chamberlain and A. Cope.

Cat 36:

Fountain-pen with detachable nib

NMI HE:1995.24 (temp.)

In early December, Lloyd George had increased the pressure on the Irish delegates when he threatened them with war within three days should they refuse to sign the *Articles of Agreement for a Treaty Between Great Britain and Ireland*.
This pen belonged to Michael Collins, and was reputedly used to sign the Treaty. Collins had been at the Laverys' house on the days before he signed and is believed by Hazel Lavery's friends to have been influenced by her in his decision to sign it.

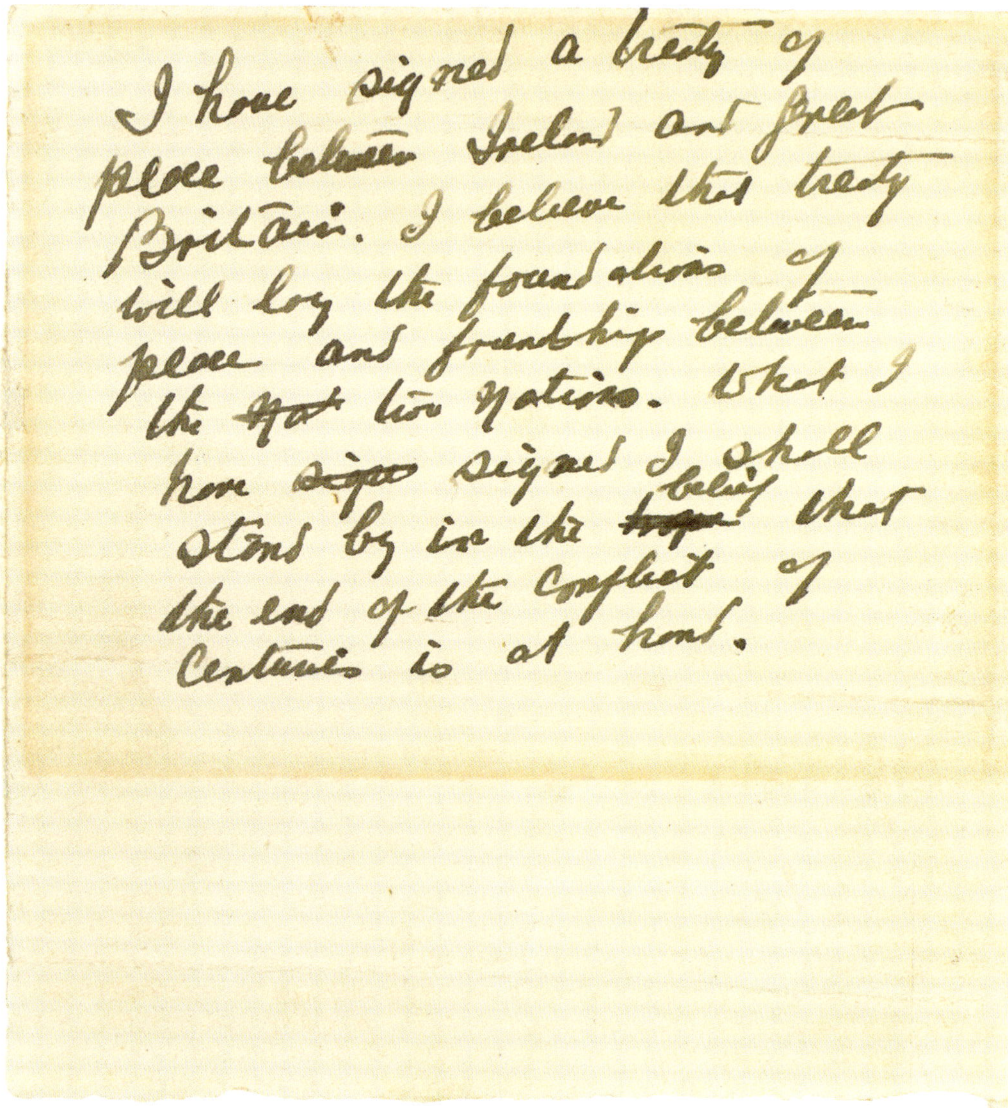

I have signed a treaty of
peace between Ireland and Great
Britain. I believe that treaty
will lay the foundations of
peace and friendship between
the two nations. What I
have signed I shall
stand by in the belief that
the end of the conflict of
centuries is at hand.

Cat 37:

Handwritten note

NMI HE:EWL.402

Arthur Griffith wrote this message for issue to the world press immediately after signing the Treaty on 6 December 1921. It reads: 'I have signed a treaty of peace between Ireland and Great Britain. I believe that treaty will lay the foundations of peace and friendship between the two nations. What I have signed I shall stand by in the belief that the end of the conflict of centuries is at hand.'

AFTERMATH
DECEMBER 1921 – SPRING 1922

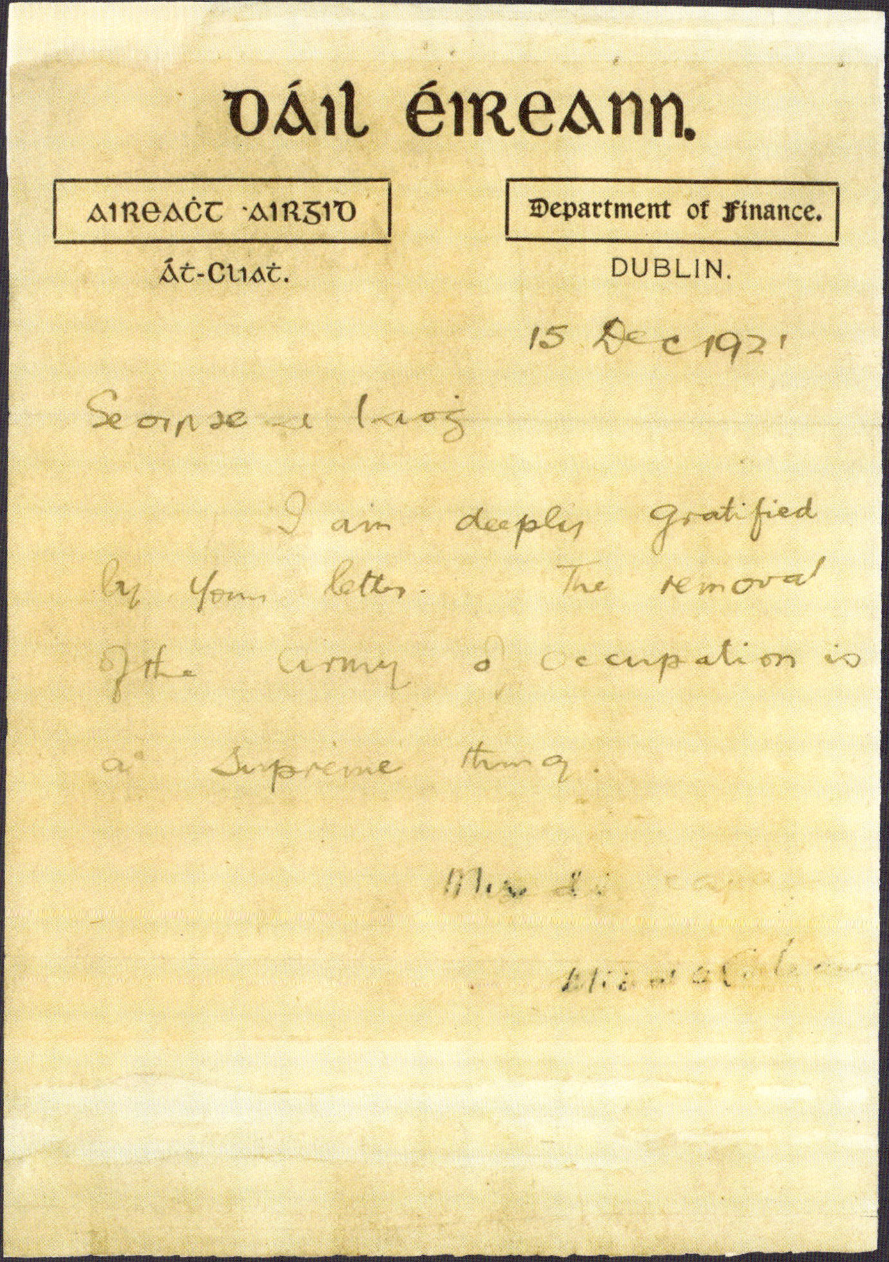

DÁIL ÉIREANN.

AIREAĊT AIRGIḊ | Department of Finance.

ÁT-CLIAT. | DUBLIN.

15 Dec 1921

Seoirse a Laoġ

I am deeply gratified by your letter. The removal of the army of occupation is a supreme thing.

Mise le ...

Cat 38:

Letter, 15 December 1921

NMI HE:EW.5764

Upon his return to Dublin, Michael Collins wrote to Seoirse a Laoġ (George Lyons): 'The removal of the army of occupation is a supreme thing'. Collins was referring to the evacuation of the British Army, which began in January 1922 and ended with the hand-over of the Royal Barracks, Dublin (today called Collins Barracks, housing the National Museum of Ireland – Decorative Arts & History) on 17 December 1922.

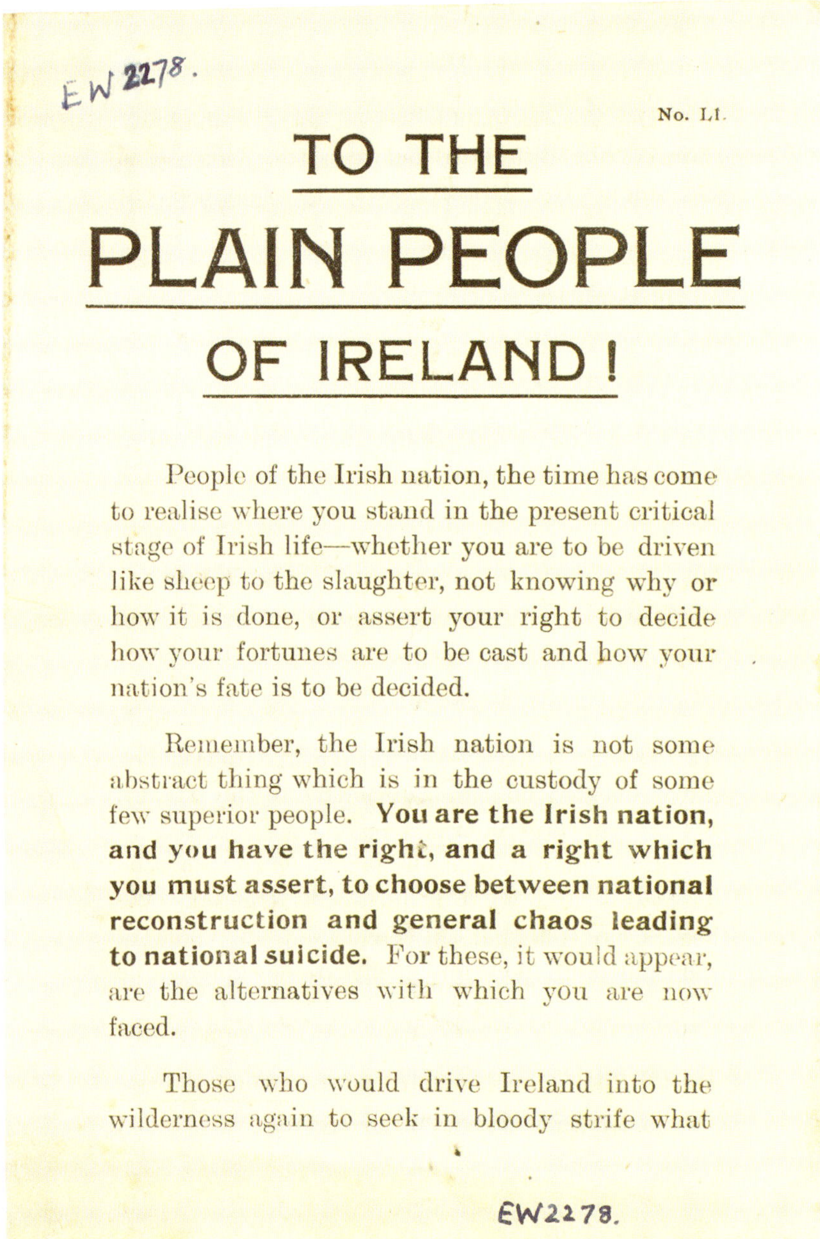

EW 2278.

No. LI.

TO THE PLAIN PEOPLE OF IRELAND!

People of the Irish nation, the time has come to realise where you stand in the present critical stage of Irish life—whether you are to be driven like sheep to the slaughter, not knowing why or how it is done, or assert your right to decide how your fortunes are to be cast and how your nation's fate is to be decided.

Remember, the Irish nation is not some abstract thing which is in the custody of some few superior people. **You are the Irish nation, and you have the right, and a right which you must assert, to choose between national reconstruction and general chaos leading to national suicide.** For these, it would appear, are the alternatives with which you are now faced.

Those who would drive Ireland into the wilderness again to seek in bloody strife what

EW2278.

Cat 39:

Pro-Treaty propaganda handbill, reprinted from the gazette Éire Óg, 25 February 1922

NMI HE:EW.2278

This four-page leaflet defends the Treaty and those who accepted it, not as 'the end of the nation's battle, but (...) the means by which to advance to whatever goal the country's interests demand'. It argues that the Treaty provides 'the vital substances which give life, strength and stability to a people', including control of revenue, industry, agriculture and education. It accuses anti-Treatyists as offering 'no sane alternative' and as being 'devoted to clouding the minds of the people'.

The historical collections of the National Museum of Ireland include pro-Treaty propaganda handbills from 1922, many of which were transferred to the Museum from the National Library of Ireland in 1981. These handbills were usually printed using red and black ink. A number of them outline the perceived freedom and advantages of the Treaty — in contrast to remaining within the British Empire. Some also home in on particular topics such as the Oath of Allegiance to the British Crown, or they appeal to Irish people to support the Treaty and the newly won right to self-determination.

Most of the anti-Treaty handbills were donated to the Museum by individuals in the past. They often aim to appeal to the political conscience of Irish people and of the individual reader, reminding them of the struggle for an Irish Republic in the past. The Republic is portrayed as the only accepted way of self-determination and Ireland would be 'in danger' until it has been established.

Both pro- and anti-Treaty sides used evocative, emotional and at times derogatory language in these handbills. A recurring feature is a statement on the bottom of the one-page handbills from both sides, pointing out that they were printed on 'Irish paper', using 'Irish ink' and 'Irish labour'.

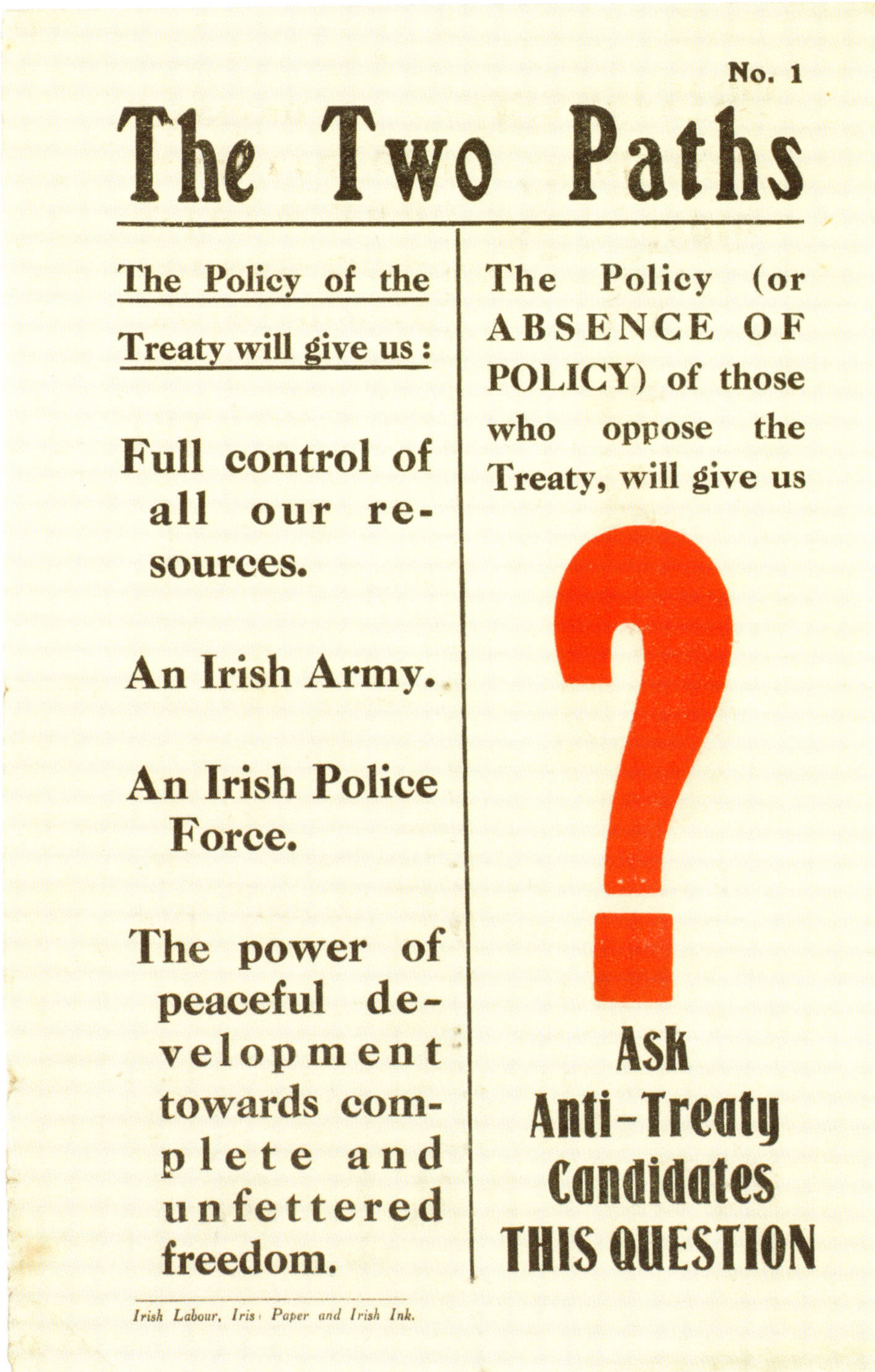

Cat 40:

Pro-Treaty propaganda handbill, 1922

NMI HE:EW.3486

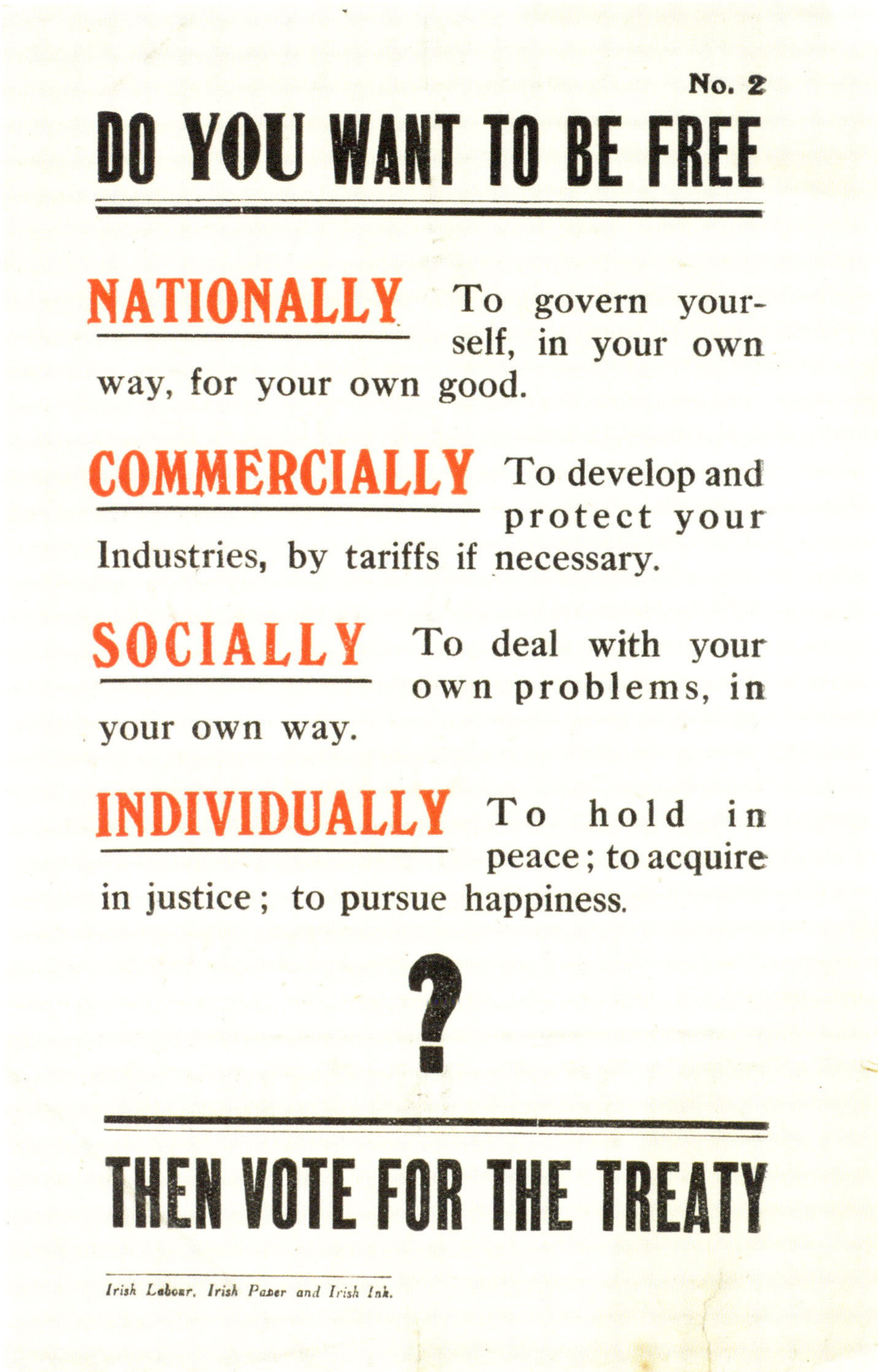

No. 2

DO YOU WANT TO BE FREE

NATIONALLY To govern yourself, in your own way, for your own good.

COMMERCIALLY To develop and protect your Industries, by tariffs if necessary.

SOCIALLY To deal with your own problems, in your own way.

INDIVIDUALLY To hold in peace; to acquire in justice; to pursue happiness.

?

THEN VOTE FOR THE TREATY

Irish Labour, Irish Paper and Irish Ink.

Cat 41:

Pro-Treaty propaganda handbill, 1922

NMI HE:EW.3488

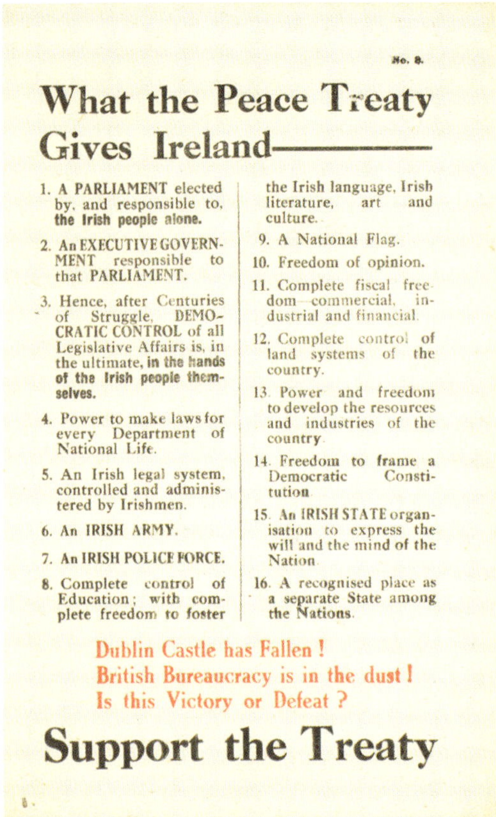

No. 8.

What the Peace Treaty Gives Ireland——

1. A PARLIAMENT elected by, and responsible to, **the Irish people alone.**
2. An EXECUTIVE GOVERNMENT responsible to that PARLIAMENT.
3. Hence, after Centuries of Struggle, DEMOCRATIC CONTROL of all Legislative Affairs is, in the ultimate, **in the hands of the Irish people themselves.**
4. Power to make laws for every Department of National Life.
5. An Irish legal system, controlled and administered by Irishmen.
6. An IRISH ARMY.
7. An IRISH POLICE FORCE.
8. Complete control of Education; with complete freedom to foster the Irish language, Irish literature, art and culture.
9. A National Flag.
10. Freedom of opinion.
11. Complete fiscal freedom—commercial, industrial and financial.
12. Complete control of land systems of the country.
13. Power and freedom to develop the resources and industries of the country.
14. Freedom to frame a Democratic Constitution.
15. An IRISH STATE organisation to express the will and the mind of the Nation.
16. A recognised place as a separate State among the Nations.

Dublin Castle has Fallen!
British Bureaucracy is in the dust!
Is this Victory or Defeat?

Support the Treaty

Cat 42:

Pro-Treaty propaganda handbill,
1922

NMI HE:EW.5315

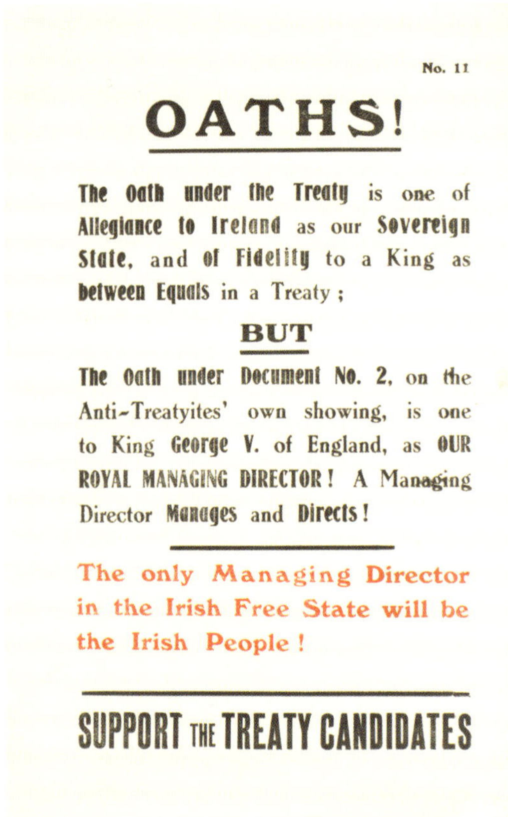

No. 11

OATHS!

The Oath under the Treaty is one of **Allegiance to Ireland** as our **Sovereign State**, and **of Fidelity** to a King as **between Equals** in a Treaty;

BUT

The Oath under Document No. 2, on the Anti-Treatyites' own showing, is one to King **George V.** of England, as **OUR ROYAL MANAGING DIRECTOR!** A Managing Director **Manages** and **Directs!**

The only Managing Director in the Irish Free State will be the Irish People!

SUPPORT THE TREATY CANDIDATES

Cat 43:

Pro-Treaty propaganda handbill,
1922

NMI HE:EW.3487

Cat 44:

> **Pro-Treaty propaganda handbill,**
1922, No. 19

NMI HE.EW.5186

This Irish-language handbill is urging people to vote for the Treaty:
It translates as: 'Two years ago the Irish Free State was the same as Irish Freedom. Now, according to Childers and similar Gaels, it is Irish slavery and exactly what England wants. Who will take the word of the English over the word of the Irish on what is freedom. Vote for the Free State.'

Uimh. 19

DHÁ BHLIAIN Ó SHIN DOB IONANN

Saorstát na hEireann

agus

Saoirse na hEireann

Anois, dar le Childers agus le "Gaedhil" eile dá shórt is ionann é agus

DAOIRSE na hEIREANN

an rud díreach a theastuigheann ó Shasana.

Cé thógfaidh focal an tSasanaigh thar focal an Eireannaigh ar cad is

SAOIRSE

ann

BHÓTÁIL LEIS AN

SAORSTÁT.

Páipeur Gaedhlach, Dubhach Gaedhlach, Saothar Ceárd-Chumainn Ghaedhlaigh.

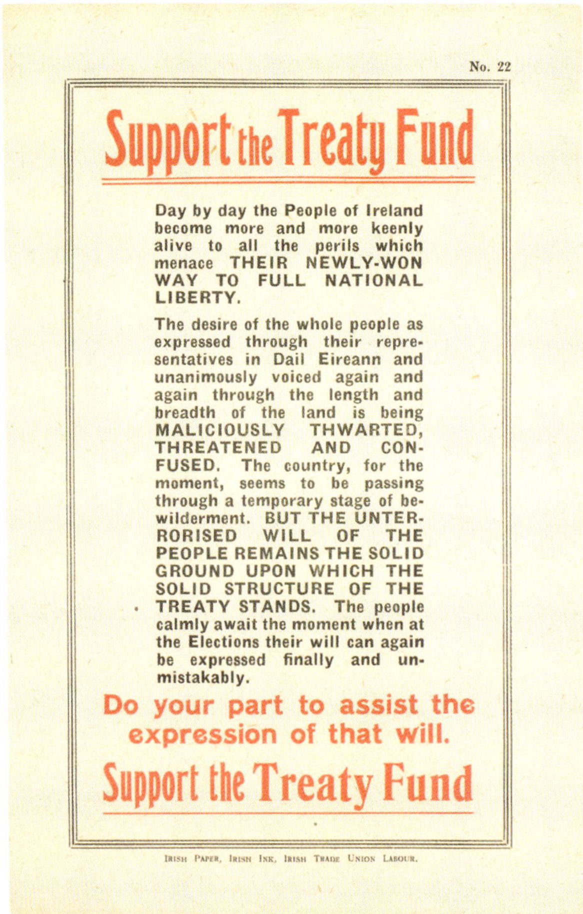
No. 22

Support the Treaty Fund

Day by day the People of Ireland become more and more keenly alive to all the perils which menace THEIR NEWLY-WON WAY TO FULL NATIONAL LIBERTY.

The desire of the whole people as expressed through their representatives in Dail Eireann and unanimously voiced again and again through the length and breadth of the land is being MALICIOUSLY THWARTED, THREATENED AND CONFUSED. The country, for the moment, seems to be passing through a temporary stage of bewilderment. BUT THE UNTERRORISED WILL OF THE PEOPLE REMAINS THE SOLID GROUND UPON WHICH THE SOLID STRUCTURE OF THE TREATY STANDS. The people calmly await the moment when at the Elections their will can again be expressed finally and unmistakably.

Do your part to assist the expression of that will.

Support the Treaty Fund

Irish Paper, Irish Ink, Irish Trade Union Labour.

Cat 45:

Pro-Treaty election handbill, 1922

NMI HE:EW.5185

The reader is asked to support the pro-Treaty side ahead of the 1922 elections. 'The country, for the moment, seems to be passing through a temporary stage of bewilderment. But the unterrorised will of the people remains the solid ground upon which the solid structure of the Treaty stands (...)'

Cat 46:

> **Pamphlet: *Clause by Clause*,** 1922

NMI HE:EW.1122.4

In this publication, Erskine Childers outlines the key differences between the 'Articles of Agreement' in the Anglo-Irish Treaty and de Valera's Document No. 2, which de Valera put forward during the Treaty debates in the Dáil in January 1922.
Childers describes the key difference as follows: 'whereas the Treaty makes Ireland consent to inclusion in the British Empire and accept allegiance to the King of England (...), Document No. 2 leaves Ireland an Independent Republic (...), connected with the British Commonwealth of Nations by a Treaty of Association which leaves her absolutely free (...)'.
Childers opposed the Treaty and wrote this pamphlet because he believed that it was 'of the utmost importance to show to the people of Ireland what Document No 2 is (...) and why it is (...) an honourable alternative to the "Treaty"'.

No. 8.

CLAUSE BY CLAUSE

A Comparison between "The Treaty" and Document No. 2

BY

ERSKINE CHILDERS

ONE PENNY

P.T.D.

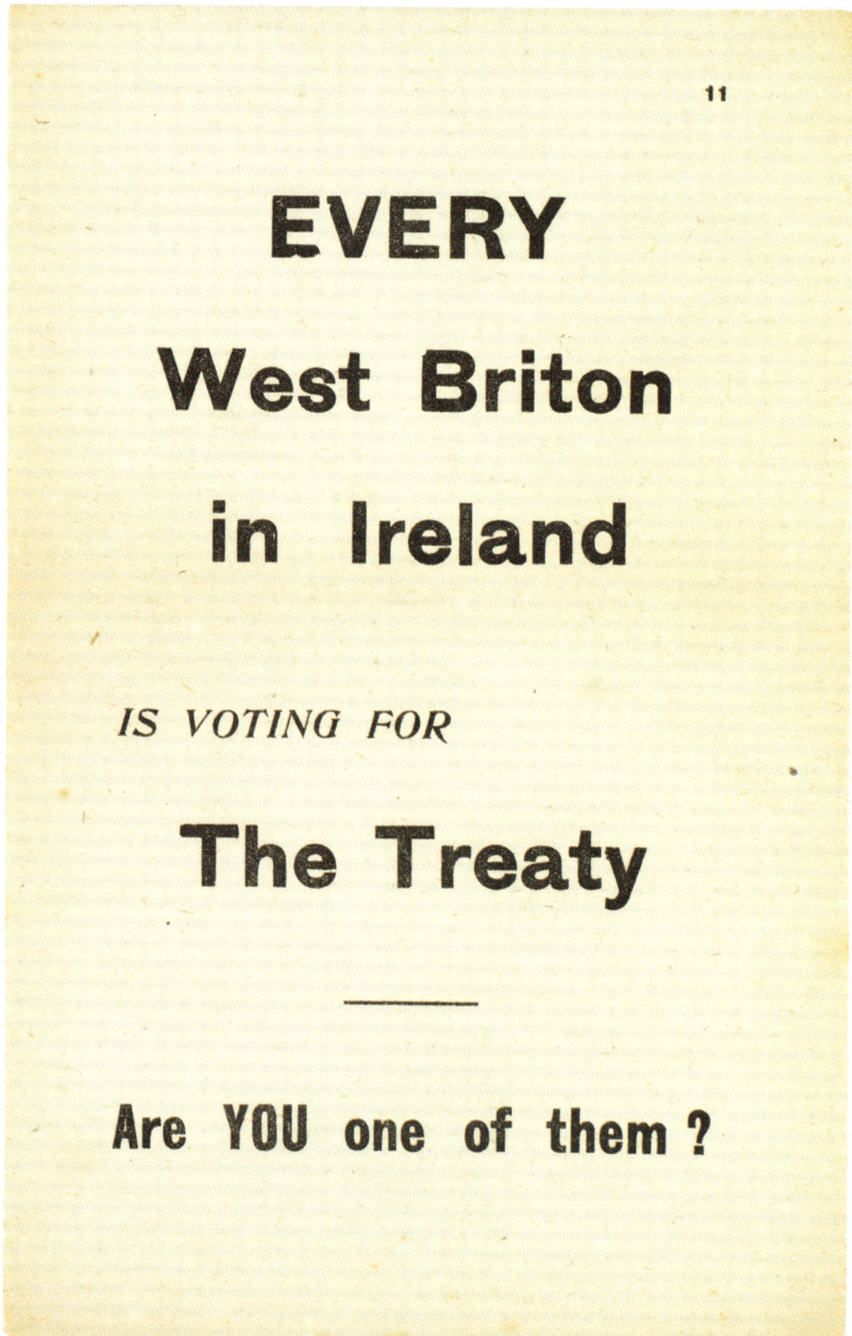

Cat 47:

Anti-Treaty propaganda handbill, 1922

NMI HE:EW.852a.13

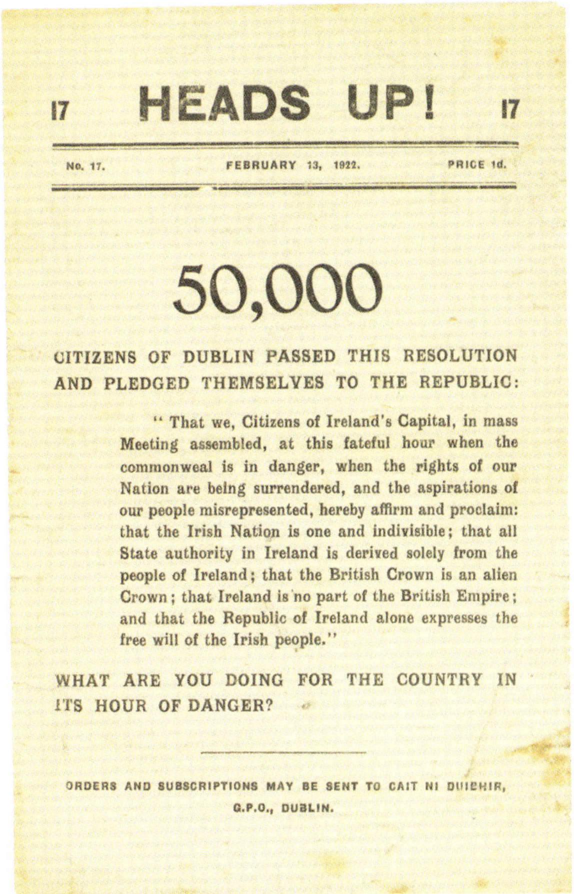

17 HEADS UP! 17

No. 17. FEBRUARY 13, 1922. PRICE 1d.

50,000

CITIZENS OF DUBLIN PASSED THIS RESOLUTION AND PLEDGED THEMSELVES TO THE REPUBLIC:

"That we, Citizens of Ireland's Capital, in mass Meeting assembled, at this fateful hour when the commonweal is in danger, when the rights of our Nation are being surrendered, and the aspirations of our people misrepresented, hereby affirm and proclaim: that the Irish Nation is one and indivisible; that all State authority in Ireland is derived solely from the people of Ireland; that the British Crown is an alien Crown; that Ireland is no part of the British Empire; and that the Republic of Ireland alone expresses the free will of the Irish people."

WHAT ARE YOU DOING FOR THE COUNTRY IN ITS HOUR OF DANGER?

ORDERS AND SUBSCRIPTIONS MAY BE SENT TO CAIT NI DUIBHIR, G.P.O., DUBLIN.

Cat 48:

Anti-Treaty propaganda handbill, 13 February 1922

NMI HE:EWT.435

This is no. 17 in a series of anti-Treaty propaganda handbills, which were issued daily and are entitled 'Heads up!' It states that 'the British Crown is an alien Crown (...) and that the Republic of Ireland alone expresses the free will of the Irish people'. It is also a call to action, asking 'What are you doing for the country in its hour of danger?'

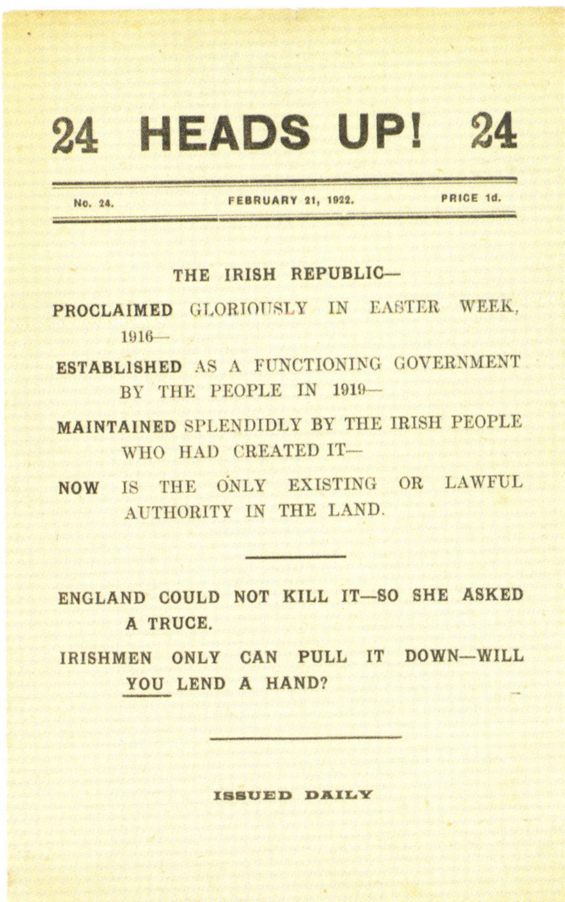

24 HEADS UP! 24

No. 24. FEBRUARY 21, 1922. PRICE 1d.

THE IRISH REPUBLIC—

PROCLAIMED GLORIOUSLY IN EASTER WEEK, 1916—

ESTABLISHED AS A FUNCTIONING GOVERNMENT BY THE PEOPLE IN 1919—

MAINTAINED SPLENDIDLY BY THE IRISH PEOPLE WHO HAD CREATED IT—

NOW IS THE ONLY EXISTING OR LAWFUL AUTHORITY IN THE LAND.

ENGLAND COULD NOT KILL IT—SO SHE ASKED A TRUCE.

IRISHMEN ONLY CAN PULL IT DOWN—WILL YOU LEND A HAND?

ISSUED DAILY

Cat 49:

Anti-Treaty propaganda handbill, 21 February 1922

NMI HE:EWT.432

This handbill describes the Irish Republic as 'the only existing or lawful authority in the land' and urges the reader to 'maintain' it [by opposing the Treaty].

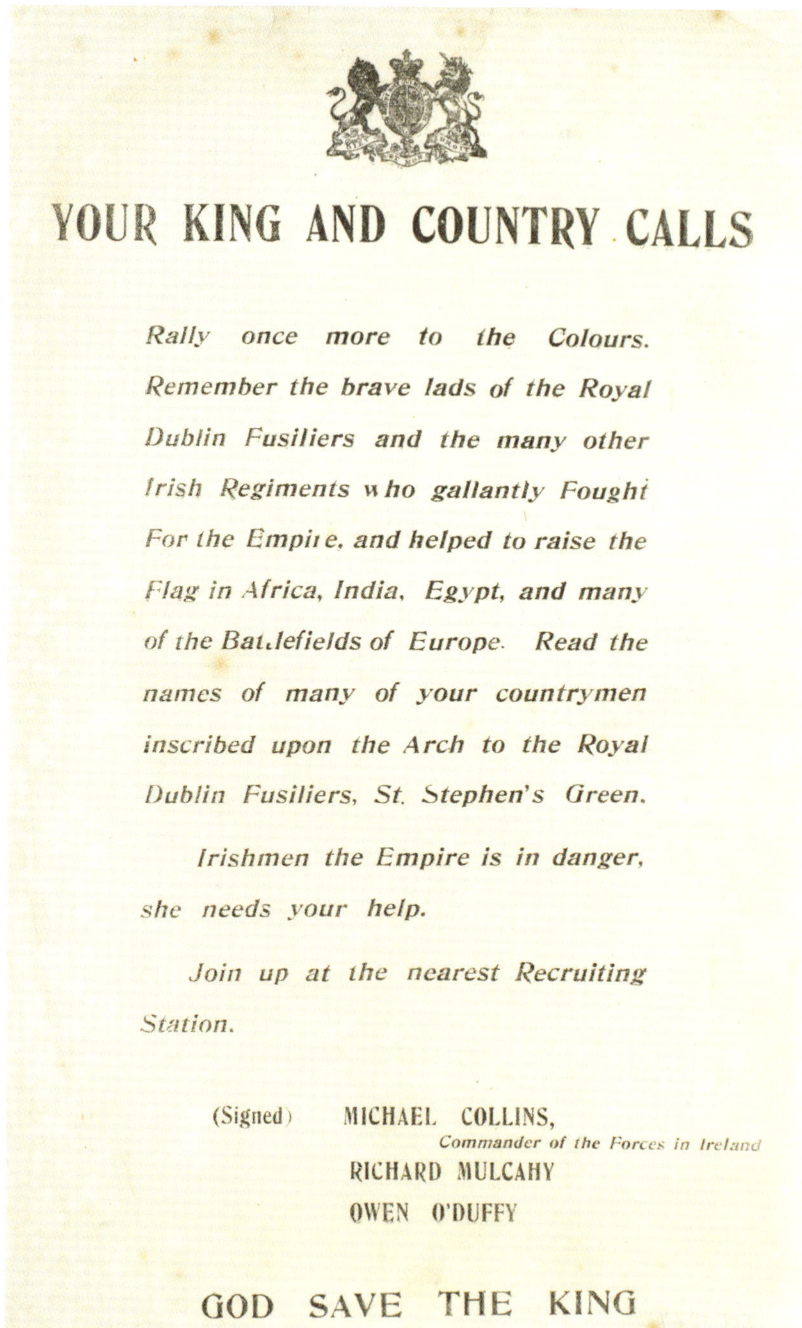

YOUR KING AND COUNTRY CALLS

Rally once more to the Colours. Remember the brave lads of the Royal Dublin Fusiliers and the many other Irish Regiments who gallantly Fought For the Empire, and helped to raise the Flag in Africa, India, Egypt, and many of the Battlefields of Europe. Read the names of many of your countrymen inscribed upon the Arch to the Royal Dublin Fusiliers, St. Stephen's Green.

Irishmen the Empire is in danger, she needs your help.

Join up at the nearest Recruiting Station.

(Signed) MICHAEL COLLINS,
Commander of the Forces in Ireland
RICHARD MULCAHY
OWEN O'DUFFY

GOD SAVE THE KING

Cat 50:

Anti-Treaty propaganda handbill, 1922

NMI HE:EW.1927

This small poster has been designed as a mock call to arms for the British Empire. It portrays Treaty supporters Michael Collins, Richard Mulcahy and Eoin O'Duffy as Commanders of the British forces.

THE ARMY OF THE SOUTH

Is United under Liam Lynch

in Defence of

THE REPUBLIC.

Men of Dublin

WHERE DO YOU STAND?

With the English Allies

Or with a United South of

Ireland?

Cat 51:

Anti-Treaty propaganda handbill

NMI HE:EW.939.49

1921
LONDON
DEC 6
NA CURU
ATA TAITH-
MECHTA LA
FEINE
CUIR INDLISTECA...
BEIM NAILLECH
NAD NERTAD
TUATHA.
SENCHUS MOR
Contracts which are
Dissolved by the
FENI.....
Taking an Oath
which the
country
does not
confirm

Cat 52:

The 'Treaty' page of *Leabhar na hAiséirghe (Book of the Resurrection)* by Art O'Murnaghan, *c.* 1947

NMI HE:EW.1626

Leabhar na hAiséirghe or *The Book of the Resurrection* was created by the self-taught artist Art O'Murnaghan between 1924 and 1951, and was one of the most brilliant works of visual art of the Celtic Revival. The 27 vellum pages of the illuminated manuscript were intended to honour the memory of the dead of the Irish independence struggle. The 'Treaty Page' incorporates a map of Ireland as its central motif, and depicts the pen used to sign the Treaty in a symbolic location between the Irish Tricolour flag and the constituent flags of the British 'Union Jack' (top, centre of the artwork).

BIOGRAPHIES

Dr Edith Andrees is a cultural historian and curator of the metalwork, numismatics and scientific instruments collections at the National Museum of Ireland–Decorative Arts & History. She has worked in museums in Germany and Ireland since 1999, and lectured at the European University Viadrina in Germany and at University College Dublin. Her research interests include historical narratives and their accessibility in museums. Since 2013 she has worked on a number of participative arts and history projects for the Irish Decade of Centenaries programme, which have addressed themes of interdisciplinary research and historical memory. Alongside Logan Sisley, she is co-curator of the exhibition *Studio & State: The Laverys and the Anglo-Irish Treaty*, on which this publication is based.

Fintan Cullen is Professor Emeritus of History of Art at the University of Nottingham. He has published many books and essays on the political dimension of Irish art and colonialism. He recently co-edited, with Róisín Kennedy, *Sources in Irish art 2* (Cork University Press, 2021).

Born in the UK, **David Godbold** studied at Goldsmiths' College, University of London, in the mid-1980s before moving to Ireland in 1990. Since then he has been immersed in Irish visual arts, working as a practising and exhibiting artist and as a lecturer in painting at the National College of Art and Design, Dublin, for over a decade. Since being awarded a Ph.D in Fine Art and Visual Communication in 2007, he has also been writing on art and polemics and is a Director of Mother's Tankstation, Dublin/London. He lives and works in Dublin and County Wexford.

Niamh McCann's work proffers a considered, individual voice in contemporary Irish art, effortlessly correlating strands of three-dimensional work, painting/drawing and installation. This in itself is unpredictable and frequently humorous, most immediate in the playful use of appropriated political figuration in her body of work *Furtive Tears*. Layering and re-coding the given image, figure or cultural trope, a quasi-deified equilibrium is achieved when juxtaposed with globalised cultural imagery. Her work is represented in the collections of the Irish Museum of Modern Art; Limerick City Gallery; Swansea City Council; the London Institute; Hiscox, London; and the Hugh Lane Gallery.

Dr Sinéad McCoole is the author of many books, including *Hazel: a life of Lady Lavery*, and curator of the *Lady Lavery—Society and Politics* (1996) and *Passion and Politics—The Salon Revisited* (2010) exhibitions at the Hugh Lane Gallery. She was Historical Advisor for the Ireland 2016 Centenary Programme and curated the centenary exhibitions *Mná 1916–2016* and *100 Years of Women in Politics and Public Life* (2018). She is a member of the Expert Advisory Group on the Government of Ireland Decade of Centenaries Programme and an *ex officio* member of Vótáil100.

Fearghal McGarry is Professor of Modern Irish History at Queen's University Belfast and a member of the Royal Irish Academy. His books include *The Abbey rebels of 1916: a lost revolution* (Gill and Macmillan, 2015) and *The Rising. Ireland: Easter 1916* (Oxford University Press, 2016 edn). He recently co-edited *Ireland 1922: independence, partition and civil war* (Royal Irish Academy) and *The Irish revolution: a global history* (NYU Press). He is a member of the National Museum of Ireland's Expert Advisory Group, which is advising the Museum on the development of its 20th Century History of Ireland Galleries.

Mick O'Dea is a past President of the Royal Hibernian Academy and a member of Aosdána since 1996. He has served on the Board of Governors of the National Gallery of Ireland, and is currently the chairman of the Stamp Design Advisory Committee and a member of the Philatelic Advisory Committee of An Post. In addition, he is a Fellow of the Anatomical Society, an honorary member of the Royal Scottish Academy and a board member of the Ballinglin Arts Foundation. He has extensive previous experience of lecturing in various art colleges in Ireland, the UK and the USA. He left full-time employment in 1999 to finally concentrate fully on his art. He has been exhibiting since 1977 and has been the recipient of numerous awards. His work can be found in many public and private collections.

Logan Sisley was born in Aotearoa New Zealand, where he studied art history at the University of Otago, Dunedin, and then at the University of Auckland. He moved to Scotland in 2000 and worked for the National Library of Scotland, the National Galleries of Scotland and the Edinburgh College of Art. From 2007 he was Exhibitions Curator at the Hugh Lane Gallery, where he is now Acting Head of Collections. He curated *The Art of Negotiation: John Lavery's Anglo-Irish Treaty Portraits* at the Embassy of Ireland, London, in October–November 2021.

ACKNOWLEDGEMENTS

The National Museum of Ireland and Hugh Lane Gallery wish to thank the following individuals and institutions who in various ways have helped to bring this exhibition and publication together: Peter Belling, Denise Byrne, Joe Byrne, Yvonne Doherty, Lucia Fabbro, Paul Heary, Sandra Heise, Raffaella Lanino, Brenda Malone, Fearghal McGarry, Ellen McKeever, Kate Moriarty, Jessica O'Donnell, Mary O'Dowd, Philip Roe, Lorna Rowley, Bryan Rutledge, Billy Shortall, Valerie Stone, Federica Traversa, Alex Ward, Richard Weinacht, Audrey Whitty, Gavin Woodruff; NMI and HLG Marketing, Education and Facilities Teams; the Office of Public Works; the lenders who generously supported the exhibition: National Gallery of Ireland, National Museums Northern Ireland, and Defence Forces Ireland's Military Archives; and the essayists: Logan Sisley, Edith Andrees, Fearghal McGarry, Sinéad McCoole, Fintan Cullen, Mick O'Dea, David Godbold and Niamh McCann.

IMAGE CREDITS

Unless otherwise stated all images of Hugh Lane Gallery collection artworks are © Hugh Lane Gallery and all images of National Museum of Ireland objects are © National Museum of Ireland. Other images as follows: pp. iv, 42, 45, 48, 55, 72: image © National Portrait Gallery, London; p. 24: image © Getty Images; pp. 27, 103, 104: photo © National Gallery of Ireland; p. 30: image courtesy of the Jackie Clarke Collection; p. 33: image © Glasgow Museums; p. 35: image © Fitzwilliam Museum, Cambridge; p. 46: Album / Alamy Stock Photo; p. 47: Mauritius Images/ TopFoto; pp. 54, 57: image © Illustrated London News Ltd/Mary Evans; pp. 62 (Cardinal Michael Logue) and p. 65 (James Craig), 102: image © National Museums Northern Ireland; p. 64: Royal Academy of Arts; p. 66: image © The Fine Art Society, London, UK / Bridgeman Images; p. 68: image © Imperial War Museum; p. 69: (Seán Keating) © IVARO; (Diego Velázquez) image © Photographic Archive Museo Nacional del Prado; p. 70: image courtesy of St Patrick's Parish, Donegall Street, Belfast; p. 74: image courtesy of National Library of Ireland; p. 118 (rubber stamp): image © Military Archives.